MW00944171

"If you are parent whos‹   ₁g
relationships with your ch   ₁n
both child and parent, Gr   ₁t
Guide to Relief, is your .... ₁ₒ₁ ₛᵤ𝚌𝚌ₑₛₛ. ₁₁ ₁𝚝 𝚞regory demonstrates
how keeping our attention on the key driver of a successful relationship with
our children, our relationship with ourselves, creates not only well adjusted
children, but adults as well. When you dive into her story you will see your
own struggles reflected. If you absorb her practical advice, you will learn
how to move through those struggles and into the understanding necessary
to make you a powerful, peaceful and loving parent."

Doreen Banaszak, Coach, Teacher
and Author of *Excuse Me, Your Life is Now.*

Terri Gregory wraps you in her warm embrace with an equal mix of heart
and sass. The six children who became hers after a tragic accident were
blessed to find her and so are we. This incredible story will touch and guide
your own parenting heart.

Tami Lynn Kent, MSPT and author of *Mothering
From Your Center* and *Wild Feminine.*

Terri Gregory is funny, brave, and wise. She's earned her insight through
heart and hard work. Her stories make us feel less isolated as parents.

Ariel Gore, Editor of Hip Mama

I have seen magic occur in Terri's workshops. Her sense-making strategies
are founded in sound research and delivered with humor.

Mary Jean Sandall, Educational Leadership Coach
and Retired Principal.

This book clarifies the fine line between guiding my children and "doing
it for them." The clear and conscious guidelines balanced with stories
and experiences help make it all so clear. This book has transformed
understanding into powerful actions. Happy mamma and happy kiddos!

Rev. Liliana Barzola Read,
Lotus Lantern Healing Arts

The Identity Crisis of Parenting

A Short Guide to Relief

TERRI GREGORY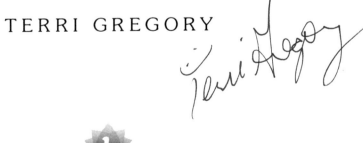

BALBOA
PRESS
A DIVISION OF HAY HOUSE

Balboa Press books may be ordered through booksellers or by contacting:

Balboa Press
A Division of Hay House
1663 Liberty Drive
Bloomington, IN 47403
www.balboapress.com
1-(877) 407-4847

Because of the dynamic nature of the Internet, any web addresses or links contained in this book may have changed since publication and may no longer be valid. The views expressed in this work are solely those of the author and do not necessarily reflect the views of the publisher, and the publisher hereby disclaims any responsibility for them.

The author of this book does not dispense medical advice or prescribe the use of any technique as a form of treatment for physical, emotional, or medical problems without the advice of a physician, either directly or indirectly. The intent of the author is only to offer information of a general nature to help you in your quest for emotional and spiritual well-being. In the event you use any of the information in this book for yourself, which is your constitutional right, the author and the publisher assume no responsibility for your actions.

Any people depicted in stock imagery provided by Thinkstock are models, and such images are being used for illustrative purposes only.
Certain stock imagery © Thinkstock.

Printed in the United States of America.

ISBN: 978-1-4525-8088-3 (sc)
ISBN: 978-1-4525-8090-6 (hc)
ISBN: 978-1-4525-8089-0 (e)

Library of Congress Control Number: 2013915450

Balboa Press rev. date: 9/17/2013

In Memory of Ly Xu Ha

Acknowledgements

This book has happened only because of certain people in my life who brought it about and it is to these that I owe many thanks for being my impetus and inspiration:

My kids: Tim, Oanh, Gabbie, Chau, Quy and John, the absolute kick-starters of my heart.

My writing group: Marie and Marissa. Thank you for being my loving editors and encouraging critics.

My mentors, my friends: Joyce, Mary-Jean, Kary, Sharon, and Vonnie. I have learned so much from your kindness, your goodwill and your sincerity.

My start-up editor: Nancy Marriott. Thank you for your clear and concise direction.

My editor and "baby-daddy": Wayne Gregory. Your astute assessment and heart for the subject matter is matched only by your humor and graciousness. You *know*, from beginning to end, this could not have happened without you.

My project manager(s) at Balboa: Heather Perry and her team. Thanks to you for your smarts and your compassion.

To my graphics designers: Theresa Pridemore and Chau Young.

To my mom: Miss Kelly. Thank you for teaching me very early on to see myself through the light in your eyes.

To my readers: Pat and Kitti. Thanks for the input and insight and the joy you took in this task.

To my fiancée: Mark Fancey. Thank you for encouraging and supporting my writing by holding me and by holding the space around me.

And, finally, thanks to my Lucky Stars who shine on me whether I see them or not.

Foreword

When I was a kid, I always knew that my folks did a lot for me, but it wasn't until I became a parent myself that I fully appreciated everything they had done. I knew that parenting was hard work. I had a taste of this responsibility caring for my younger siblings when I was growing up. I even delayed having kids until several years into my marriage. However, nothing prepared me for what parenthood really meant. There is no manual for being a parent. That is why I am so glad that my mom wrote this book. I feel like it's just one more thing she's done for me.

In this book, she shares her story about how she became a parent and highlights some of the lessons she learned along the way. This book is a path of self-discovery through parenting. It is about understanding how experiences shape your view of the world and of yourself. She shares honestly through her own stories and helps us see that the only change that we can make is within ourselves.

You are probably reading this book because you want to be a better parent or need help with dealing with your kid(s). I know that I do. Reading this book has helped me to better understand my kids and myself. We do learn to be better parents along the way and some of us even "fake it till we make it." I'm grateful for the chance to look back through my mom's experiences and to better understand my own past as I move into my future as a parent and, more importantly, as a person.

Grace Oanh Ellis
Mother of 3
Vancouver, Washington
April 2013

Table of Contents

Introduction
What is it that you want?

Prologue

Section 1: The Life Stages

Section 2: Identity Crisis

Section 3: How To Break the Anger Cycle

Section 4: Redefining the Word "Help"

Section 5: Tools

Section 6: Home, Hearth, Heart

Epilogue

On the Children
by Khalil Gibran

Your children are not your children.
They are the sons and daughters of Life's longing for itself.
They come through you but not from you,
And though they are with you, yet they belong not to you.

INTRODUCTION

What is it
that you want?

Why This Book?

For two decades now, as a parent and teacher, I have learned, watched, and assimilated into my own life the permission to be authentic while allowing my children and students to do the same. During this time, I have taught parents and non-parents, teachers and parole officers, case workers and teenagers affected by all of the above—basically, anyone interested in expanding what they already know to become more of who they already are. So, when I use the word "parent" please feel free to replace it with whatever role you are in presently. The main reason this book came into existence is because some of the parents I have worked with as clients, have asked for something in writing. They either wanted a reference for themselves or information they could pass on to friends. These are basic concepts that will enhance anything you're doing at home, work or school, basically anyplace where healthy relationships are necessary for positive outcomes.

While learning, using, teaching and sharing these tools, I have seen parents melt from the rigid block of icy self-flagellation and severe expectation, into warm, fluid pools of living and loving and allowing life (both their own and their children's) to flow through them.

Most people who appear in my path are those who have read the books on parenting, waited until they were "ready" to have children, given up sleep and jobs, and given and given and given, only to find themselves in a heap of confusion and sadness, often aghast at what has evolved from their best intentions. This metaphorical heap is the same place I found myself early on.

This book is, in essence, a book of self-discovery, initiated and practiced through parenting. Here, in a nutshell, are the concerns of most of us: Am I going to make it through parenthood? Is my kid going to survive my best efforts? How will my child learn to be a successful person, a contributing member of society? How will I know when this has happened? When will they move out? Will I be ready for this? Will they be ready? How do I help them? How do I keep us all afloat until then?

Parenting, like most things in life that we humans complicate, is really quite simple. Not necessarily easy, but simple. The more you know about yourself, the easier it will be to parent. No matter what your age or life-path, whether you are a prospective parent, a new parent, a grandparent, the parent of an adult or the parent of a semi-adult, it is not too late to improve on your methods, both for your sake and for the sake of your child. With the right tools and some intentional practice, you can steer yourself, and therefore your child into the vibrancy of life.

Through my own experience, and through others in which I've shared, I have come to believe that the most effective parents are those who understand and *accept* themselves. If you are a frustrated parent (and I believe all of us have been to some extent) it is possible, even probable, that you can go easy on yourself and learn to parent more freely through your willing use of the tools this book provides.

Think of it this way: an annual medical exam, a twice-yearly dental cleaning, we accept as necessary, preventive maintenance. The results of these could be additional diagnostic testing, changes in diet or methods, in essence, that which will prevent further and more serious complications and dread. The same can be said of the personal and familial alterations that can be had by the information and exercises in this book. Open your heart and mind to these things and change will follow.

In short, the theory doesn't matter as much as the practice itself does. Whether you have come to parenting through birth, adoption, marriage, as godparents, foster parents, or caregivers, what you will be doing here is creating pathways for change. This change will come through recognition of the reasons for your own operational procedures. Once you agree to take a look at why you do what you do, you will see why the child in your life responds as she does. And you will see that parenting is symptomatic of life. How you live, both within and outside of yourself, has a most definite bearing on the way in which you parent.

What we all want are healthy relationships, especially with our children. Healthy relationships involve healthy people. Any healthy relationship is mutual in give and take. It hasn't been a very popular idea, but we can only truly love and value others, when we love and value ourselves. Love is an action word. Anything we do to help ourselves, to help others, to help a situation is full-on love, unless it is done from a deficit. Loving me=loving you without expectation. In other words, my experience as a parent is just as valid and important as the experience of my child. This goes against the grain of the ubiquitous martyr style of parenting but it really is just that simple.

Sacrifice, in its simplest form, is defined as a voluntary loss. Parents are experts at this type of giving. Most of us are happy to put ourselves on the losing end for our kids' sake. Often times and over the years, this can lead to resentment. To give up something willingly, though, does not necessarily mean a loss if you can see that you are getting something that you value in return. For example, if you give up an important business meeting to go to your kid's soccer game, you must think about what *you* are getting in return. Not your kid, but you. Are you going to the game because you revel in seeing your beautiful child, this lively being, in action? Is it is an act of gratitude, a rite of thanksgiving? Are you going because you love seeing your kids smile when he sees you there? Or, are you going out of some idea that this makes you a better parent? Either way, you are getting some level of satisfaction from your decision. The game is your kid's deal. The part you play in this young life is your deal. If you can see that there has been an even exchange, then you won't become resentful or self-pitying.

What we want is peace and harmony in our lives, right? This is an inside job. What we ultimately want is to be happy. This is an inside job as well. So, this question of "what is it that you want?" will ultimately lead you back to yourself and the realization that no matter how much you want a child or an adult to think or act differently, you have no control over another's actions. This realization, this reminder of what you already know to be true, releases you from feeling you should be able to do what you cannot. You are then freed to focus on doing what you can, on saying what *you* will do or what *you* won't do in any given situation. Respect for both parties will always lead to freedom.

Moms and dads often feel like martyrs in the cause of good parenting. Many of them feel that they should lose themselves completely until one magical day when the kid is grown up. Think of the sighing, the complaining, the kvetching, all in the spirit of being a good and responsible parent. It feels to them like this off-kilter stance, this attitude of your-life-is-worth-more-than-my-life is the only way it can be, the only way it's supposed to be. The truth is that balance comes when it's a win–win, especially in parenting. The time of martyrdom and sacrifice (there is no "loss" when we understand what and why we are trading) is over. It's an old model that never really fit well. We've tried it on for generations and generations, shrugged around in it, itched and scratched, but it never really worked. It never worked because what we must do, as Jesus and many sages have implored, is to "Love your neighbor (in this case, your child) as you love yourself."

How To Use This Book

This book is divided into 6 major sections. Section 1 introduces you to the foundational premise of this work, the Stages of Life as defined by sociologist Erik Erikson. Section 2 will focus on some of the essential pieces informing our identities throughout these stages. Section 3 explains the Anger Cycle and helps to simplify this many faceted emotion. Section 4 will help you, as a parent, to take a look at ways to authentically help your child. Section 5 will provide specific tools for you to begin to use in the practice of parenting. Section 6 will suggest implements in making home-life easier to manage.

Each section is broken down by topics. There are many stories shared, which are designed to emphasize the broader point of discussion while bringing a more relaxed and enjoyable tone. I suggest that you read the book straight through as you would a poolside novel and then go back and "do" it. That being said, I realize that parents in the throes of child rearing may have little time for leisure reading. For this reason the book is designed in an easy access format. If you are desperate to find a solution to the constant yelling matches you've been having with your kid, for example, you can simply flip directly to the section on How to Break the Anger Cycle.

At the end of each chapter, there is a section called *The Bottom Line* that brings home the main idea of the chapter and helps you bring your thoughts together. This is followed by a section called *Ask Yourself,* that helps you relate this new information to your own life. Finally, *Try This* acts as a guided exercise. Here is where you have the opportunity to incorporate change by looking inside of yourself, considering options, and ultimately taking action. The page margins have room for you to make notes, jot down thoughts, and remind yourself of truths you see or questions to be asked. A journal or writing paper will be helpful as well.

The book is really a sort of workbook that acts as a guide. It offers a soul-searching, child-rearing map and a compass for your journey but the experience is solely yours. Reading it will be helpful. Doing the exercises will be life-changing.

PROLOGUE

"Good Morning Vietnam!"

I recall when I first realized how tired I had become. I was flying across the country with the three youngest of my children who were in elementary, middle and high school. We were headed home to Oregon after a lovely summer stay in North Carolina with their grandparents. We had a long layover in St. Louis where an old friend lived. An increasingly successful architect and world traveling bachelor, he picked us up in his Land Rover and whisked us to his three-story Georgian-style home. I remember climbing the beautiful curving staircase, luxuriating over the smooth, worn mahogany of the banister. Our tour of his fabulous house ended on the third floor, which was entirely his bedroom.

Light streamed in through the unsheathed windows and skylights. The big bed had no frame, just a swath of white linens, a billowing ocean of creamy down and soft pillows, a lamb's wool thrown carelessly over the tousled bedding. There was a formidable armoire, tall and imposing, beautifully carved. A few brushed nickel floor lamps, a drafting table and stool. There was nothing to clean up or straighten. I imagined a life of coming home and being able to choose whether you would or wouldn't take a bath, go out with friends, read, or simply stare at the tongue and groove ceiling.

I stood in the broad, open space in the middle of the room while the kids rushed about looking in his luxurious bathroom, plush with thick, white towels, softened all the more by their placement amid stainless steel and glass. At our host's behest, they ran down the wide, graceful stairs with him for the promised lemonade. But, I was transfixed. I could not make myself leave this room: the space, the simplicity, the comfort, the *quiet*. It felt to me like I was in heaven. Even now, this room is what I remember most about that whole summer.

I thought of that attic room all the way home, pictured myself lying in the middle of the big bed alone, sleeping, reading, sleeping again. Basking in the hushed sunlight, studying the golden motes as they floated in and out of my field of vision. In the months ahead, I was to dream of this space often. It's where I went in my head to rest from the pile-up of years of trying my best with kids and school, work, and marriage. Eventually, I began to realize my utter exhaustion which given the chaos and busyness of the previous years of tumultuous child rearing, I had never truly recognized until then.

Some people prepare for parenthood for years, some for months at least. But, I was launched into parenthood when I was 28 years old with a pre-dawn telephone call that came on the morning of August 14, 1990. I was already up and dressed and walking out of the front door of our little blue house in Baton Rouge, Louisiana that I shared with my husband, Wayne, and Tim.

I had discovered Tim in the winter of 1986 as I taught songs in English to a throng of black-haired, brown-eyed children. Their Vietnamese, Laotian, and Cambodian parents struggled to grasp the new language in adjacent classrooms of the old abandoned church, resurrected for this specific purpose. My classroom was full of bright-eyed elementary and preschoolers, singing at the tops of their lungs and giggling as they learned to clap and shout in the proper places. Like going to school on the weekdays, these Sunday evenings were a highlight for them.

Not so for Tim whose attendance was sporadic. At 13, he was by far the oldest there and while his 3 little sisters sat eagerly in the front row, he sometimes came in and stood against the far back wall of the classroom draped in an oversized grey trench coat, sweeping black bangs and a slack smile.

The first time he came into the classroom, it took his answering a polite "yes" to just 3 questions for me to realize how little English he knew despite his age.

"Would you like to sit down?"

"Yes," he said with a smile.

"What is your name?"

"Yes," he answered again.

"Do you understand what I'm saying?"

"Yes."

Still smiling, he walked straight out the door in what I recognized as a coping mechanism. Smiling and avoiding are common strategies while acquiring a second language via immersion in a new culture. Having had previous training in cross-culture relationships, I was neither alarmed nor offended by his actions because I knew them to be primary responses to discomfort.

What I did *not* know, however, was a lot: He was being relentlessly pursued for membership by an Asian gang at school. He was a gentle boy but full of fear and wariness. He retained the distrust for people that, along with a fighting prowess, his grandfather had instilled in him for his own protection. He was a natural artist with keen abilities and a deep capacity for learning.

What I felt for Tim was strong and immediate. I couldn't articulate the place he'd taken in my heart. I could sense his need and yet, apart from the obvious, could not define it. Being the wife of a youth minister, I had loved many kids who came in and out of our lives, but this boy's presence was like a hammer going down full force in my gut.

In the ensuing weeks I found out what I could about the family. They had been in the US for about a year, Tim had gone from third grade to fifth grade and would make the jump to eighth grade in the year following. He had four young siblings. The birth of the youngest, Quy, had caused a delay in leaving Vietnam. Quy spent his first months of life in a Philippine refugee camp with the rest of the family. It was the camp workers and teachers who had taken a liking to his older brother, Hung, and dubbed him "Tim" which remains his legal name to this day. The more I learned about him, the more I realized Tim's language and schooling deficits.

"He'll never make it," I told my husband. "He'll be transferred from grade to grade and learn little to nothing before he ages out of high school. We've got to do something, Wayne, or he'll be peeling crawfish for the rest of his life."

At the time I had no knowledge of the family's home life. I did not know that Tim was an Amerasian, or that the family he was with did not claim him as their own saying that he had been found as a baby by the mother. I did not know that the father was a mentally unstable alcoholic. I did not know that the family was able to come to the US because of Tim's status, because of the vast exodus of unwanted American GI children. I did not know that this was the mother's second husband and not the father of all of the children. I did not know that in an alcoholic rage this man woke Tim at times and beat him. I did not know that Tim had taken to sleeping with nun chucks for obvious reasons. I did not know that the man had recently been committed to the psychiatric ward for 6 weeks and was often in a drunken stupor in which he did things like urinate on the heads of his children. I did not know that it had been made clear to Tim that he would quit school as soon as possible and work so the other children, who were far more worthy, would have a chance. I did not know that Tim worked alongside his hard-working mother every day after school and on Saturdays peeling crawfish and being paid by the pound. The money, of course, went entirely to household support.

These truths and much more would be revealed to me slowly through the years and much after the fact. After it was too late for either reproach or restitution.

As I had a full time job in the commercial loan department of a large downtown bank, I took a Community ESL course on Saturdays (my only free day) and began tutoring Tim two days a week. I was desperate to see him improve. We tried to work our way through the simple curriculum but it took only a few lessons for me to realize that the language barrier was just too great.

I asked around and was directed to a Ph.D. student from Hong Kong. The gentlemanly Kenwah Wu spoke the King's English with a proper British accent. He graciously agreed to tutor Tim and continued to do so throughout the last two years of his program in astrophysics.

We enrolled Tim in a summer reading program at LSU and, thanks to Kenwah's translation and help, his parents ultimately agreed to it so long as it did not interfere with his job. Kenwah's appearance on the dark porch of the family's house had apparently made quite an impression.

During the discussion about Tim's need for education, the father went so far as to jerk his shirt down revealing a deep, red scar along his shoulder and arm in an attempt to explain why his wife worked and he could not. I was shocked and a little sickened by the angry skin and his pitiful vehemence. I could sense that he was suffering deeply and that he had suffered tremendously. I felt at once revulsion and sympathy. I knew that he was mean to Tim but at that point I did not know the extent of his cruelty. I could see that Tim was nervous throughout our visit, but I did not know until much later that his agitation stemmed from the fear that he'd be worked over after we left for causing so much trouble. But, alas, our trip had been successful.

So it was that Wayne went to the seafood plant every day that summer and young Tim, still smiling and still reeking of crawfish, would clamber into our old VW camper and putter off to yet another class. In September, his tutoring with Kenwah resumed and between the two, his language and his confidence improved greatly. He still did not trust us with family secrets, he still had deep, dark circles beneath his eyes and he still looked to have a great burden on his shoulders. But, he always seemed happy to be with us.

Toward the end of Tim's eighth grade year, he arrived at our tiny apartment for tutoring with his hand sloppily bandaged. It was under much duress and with much trepidation (he was literally shaking), that Tim told us he'd gotten hurt at work. We hadn't known that Tim had gotten a different job. Apparently, except for the 1 evening when he was tutored in our tiny living room by Kenwah, he made a seven-mile bike ride from his house to an even seedier part of town, worked until 1 or 2 a.m. in a restaurant kitchen and then rode back home to catch a bit of sleep before he got up to go to school. His thumb was numb and the unfurled bandage revealed a small but deep cut in the fat of his palm that should have had stitches if not surgery.

I was beyond appalled but Tim begged us not to tell his parents that he'd told us. He went so far as to say that if we did, he'd never come back. Kenwah seemed to understand or at least his demeanor was very calm. Wayne and I, on the other hand, were saddened and enraged by the plight of this boy we had come to cherish and began to realize the real danger he was in. We cleaned the wound, bought clean wrappings and promised Tim we would do nothing to cause him more harm. He looked as though he wanted to believe us.

In a calculated attempt, I began to call Tim's house after school and was told differing stories by his sisters, who by then I knew and loved as well. "Tim playing." "Tim sleeping." "Tim not home." Their sweet voices were timid and unsure causing my heart to break. They were as afraid as he was. Eventually, as I had hoped, his parents told him he'd have to quit work so they would not get into trouble. They were encouraged by the fact that he could legally quit school after his August birthday thus allowing him to work full time. I knew we had to act quickly. Again, we enlisted the help of Kenwah.

On a balmy summer day, Kenwah called from our house to tell Tim's parents that we were coming to ask about his moving in with us. He assured them that they would continue to get food stamps and assistance for Tim even though he would not be living with them. Tim was afraid and also excited. He was noticeably uncomfortable with the idea but at the same time very hopeful.

Wayne and I were never sure what Kenwah said, exactly, but when we went to talk later that week, a large black trash bag sagged in the middle of the living room floor. In it were Tim's meager belongings, mostly used clothing. His mother had bought a few new school supplies and seemed both anxious and relieved. Even the kids seemed to exude anxiety and did not smile and sit on our laps as they usually did when we visited. In assessing the situation, I could sense the guilt Tim felt in leaving them as well as the uneasiness they felt at losing him. When we rose to leave, it was not a happy parting. There was no hugging or tears. With a bag as big as he was slung over his back, Tim left his young siblings staring after him and came to live with us in order to improve his English and quite possibly save his life.

There were lots of strings attached to Tim. Those ideas planted by his culture, by his family, by his own sense of right and wrong. We were conscious of the obvious fact that we were not Tim's parents. It was a sticky wicket as we were his guardians and yet we had no legal responsibility for him.

Those initial years with us provided the atmosphere of an incubator for Tim. There was suddenly a bit of space, physical security and a chance to rest. The constant memory for me of those times is the picture of Wayne, his arm slung around Tim's slight little shoulder as they sat together on the edge of Tim's bed in our tiny apartment. This was when Tim began to understand that he was not expected to work for his keep or to pay us back in any form, a concept wholly new to him. The idea that he would in fact survive a bout of sickness was new to him as well, that vomiting is not a sign of death as he had so often witnessed in a war-ravaged country and then in various work and refugee camps.

This was where he began to see that he did not have to fight at school, that there were other avenues. That Wayne and I were his advocates. This is where he heard for the first time that doing homework for his friends, who did not have the good fortune of "rich Americans" taking them in, was considered cheating and not an act of collaboration. This is where he learned that the dark was not to be feared and that thunder and lightning were not sent as punishment for him and that he did not have to scramble for love and acceptance. This is where he learned to stop cowering when he was afraid and rocking when he was anxious. He learned to use his words and he learned to trust that they would be heard.

Wayne and I were young, we had good hearts and lots of good energy and we did what we could do to the very ends of ourselves but there was so much that we did not know about parenting. Wayne spent countless hours and displayed a gargantuan patience. But there were obvious constraints and attitudes that baffled us as well.

For instance, Tim became belligerent and obstinate one evening when a group of church kids came to our apartment. Tim had begun going to church with us from the start. There, a group of goofy teenagers took to him like white on rice, enveloping him into their good-natured antics and into their families. But on this evening, Tim treated these kids, these friends of his, like unwanteds. His behavior was shocking to all of us as it was extremely out of character for him. After several blatant and rude acts of defiance, Wayne asked Tim if he wanted a spanking. At this point, spankings, as well as the age old question of "do you want one?" was a cultural norm. To our great surprise, Tim responded in the affirmative. So, Wayne took him into the bedroom and spanked him.

Even as I write this, I recoil. We had never had an ounce of trouble with Tim and, frankly, we were at our wits end on this evening. This time, in particular was the first time that I realized, deep down in my soul, what we were up against. I had the unarticulated sense that there was so much we did not know and wasn't at all sure where to learn it. After the spanking, Tim was happy and went on as if nothing had ever happened. At times like these, our good hearts were not enough and in our frustration we reverted back to the behaviors and attitudes we grew up with.

It would be much later that we'd realize the two things behind this baffling occurrence:

1) Tim had been so used to having us all to himself, he was very jealous of the kids coming into his space and making themselves at home, joking around with us and getting so much of our personal attention. At that point, we were clueless as to any connection or warmth that Tim may have felt for us, as he was unable to display such emotions.

2) He had been spending some weekends with a friend from church who was very close to his father; they hunted and fished and watched sports together. He often told Tim that he could not be involved in the antics of some of their friends or his daddy would "tear him up." This was said with pride and awe and although it was something that hadn't occurred since childhood, it had left a definite impression. Tim loved being with this family. He saw this as the way families worked in a sense, and thus spanking as a sort of male bonding that he had missed out on. So, he set out to have his own spanking.

In retrospect, we were at sea when it came to helping someone who had been so physically abused and emotionally neglected. That is why I will be forever grateful to the youth group of our church. All of our mistakes were buffered by this group who bonded with Tim, took him in and generally gave him a sense of belonging among peers, which is so important to an adolescent and something that adults cannot do for them. Not only did he have his own personal English immersion program, he made great gains in cultural norms as well. At times, their honesty was brutal. I'll never forget one of the boys telling me that after a whole weekend at his house, Tim was finally able to manage "direct aim" in the bathroom. He laughed saying he had grown tired of cleaning up after Tim and kept insisting, "No, dude, the rim is *not* okay."

Every Sunday, after church, we went to Wayne's parents' big, comfortable house. Sunday lunch was always a formal affair with tablecloth and napkins on the large dining room table, and a bodacious meal cooked and served by his mother. She often served whipped cream with whatever pie or cobbler or cake we had for dessert and Tim quickly became fond of and even asked for more "white stuff." The graciousness of Wayne's parents cannot be overstated. This, too, provided a balm for Tim although, for a long while, he wasn't quite sure how to respond.

As for my mom, she pulled Tim into a tight hug on their first meeting as she had done countless children. To his great delight, Tim quickly saw that she was a kidder. To this day, when Tim calls her, he pretends to be someone else, a salesman or someone who can help her earn money to give to her very deserving grandson, but she always knows it's him and they both have a good laugh.

As well, my mother came with a passel of grandchildren of varying ages who all embraced Tim as the newest member of the family—even to the extent of my sweet nephew, Brent, getting into a fight with another 10-year old at their church when Tim visited there. During the service, a friend of Brent's made a snide remark about the "Chinese boy." A tussle ensued as Brent responded, right before he swung, "Don't talk about my cousin like that."

Wayne and I often talked about adopting Tim but this was something that his mother was unwilling to discuss; she grew visibly uncomfortable if we brought it up. In the two years that Tim was with us, she and the five kids (she'd had another baby by then) were involved with a Vietnamese congregation, giving them a much needed social outlet and sense of community. The two older girls asked us to come to their baptism and afterwards we brought them with us to Sunday lunch at "Grandma's" for the first time. Tim, without our prodding, had called Wayne's parents "Grandma" and "Grandpa" from the very beginning. Both educators, they were greatly impressed with Tim's dedication to his schoolwork. He always had homework to do after lunch and into the evening and they were happily available to help with projects or papers.

Tim continued to thrive. We had his siblings over when we could for sleepovers or Easter egg hunts, he was able to buy them gifts for Christmas and their birthdays. Wayne taught him to play tennis, which later helped him win a scholarship to college. His increasing comfort with us was balanced by a ballast of guilt about leaving his siblings and his mom behind.

On August the 13th of 1990, Tim's 18th birthday, my husband of seven years sat with me across the wide mahogany desk of my ob/gyn.

"Everything appears normal," the doctor said smiling. "But since you haven't been successful after two years of trying, we'll need to do some testing." He looked directly at me, "the first thing we'll need to do is to have your tubes blown."

Tubes blown? *My* tubes blown!?!? I immediately pictured myself hoisted by white clad technicians to a straddle position atop an upright Black & Decker leaf blower. Wayne, on the other hand, was simply to have his semen tested. It was Thursday. We had one week to prepare ourselves.

It wasn't as if I had ever had a burning desire to conceive and bear. I didn't. In fact, there were several times during the two years prior when I would sit in the bathroom with another EPT stick gone pink and wonder why I wasn't broken hearted. I mean I had heard the stories of infertile couples who clung to each other for strength, who called in sick because one needed the other for yet another code pink. And here I sat month after month glibly tossing sticks into the wastebasket, pulling on my nylons, my biggest worry of the day being whether to bring my lunch or eat out.

I did actually manage to cry once there toward the end of year two. But these were not tears of a woman stricken by her barrenness. I was afraid something was wrong with me because I *wasn't* stricken. I loved kids. I wanted kids. I had been taking care of babies practically since I had been one myself. My husband had always planned to have what he referred to as "wombs," those who came from my body, and "zooms," those who came to us by special delivery. I, on the other hand, was perfectly content to have them all come by airmail.

Maybe I'm not motherly. Perhaps my maternal heart is missing. I must have been in the wrong heart line in Heaven. I thought I was in the "mother" line and it turns out I was in the "other" line. Maybe I had mistakenly been in the cold-hearted, CEO, dragon-lady line and not the cozy, apron-wearing, cookie-baking queue. Maybe I was a lesbian. Maybe I actually hated men and didn't know it. Maybe I secretly hated kids! I LOVE kids! I am totally comfortable with kids! I want kids! Then, why don't I care about being pregnant?

The tears came that morning from this question, from not knowing, from not having answers. For me, this was the only unacceptable facet of the whole stick-y process. Even then, I had to squeeze laboriously and finally think of my grandchildless in-laws to start the cheek-rollers, kind of like an actress concentrating on shooting the 12th crying scene in a row. *No, the truth is I am softhearted, caring, maternal. I love to love.*

Tim was still sleeping on the following morning, the morning of the phone call. We had been out late the night before with friends to celebrate his birthday. School would be starting in just two weeks and he was taking a well-deserved summer break in anticipation of the 4–5 hours of homework he'd (we'd) have each day to keep him current in his sophomore year. That morning, I had to be at my fairly new job as manager of a dental practice way before the beginning 7:30 appointments. We had a full schedule with no cancellations. This would keep two hygienists, two dentists, two dental assistants, me, and another receptionist going like gangbusters.

Having finished all of his coursework and working solely on his doctoral dissertation, Wayne was employed as a Teaching Assistant by day, a commercial floor buffer by night, and a minister on Wednesday evenings and weekends. His sleep was precious and little; I crept out of our bedroom so as not to wake him. Then, as I reached for the front door knob, the phone rang and in an innocent moment my life changed forever.

A mild and sad voice unknown to me said, "Are you Mrs. Terri?"

"Yes."

"I am calling from the hospital. Tim's parents have been in an accident."

"Oh, no! An accident? Are they hurt?" I was expecting to be asked to come and get them and take them home. I imagined casts and injuries. I *never* imagined what he next said to me.

"Yes mam. I am sorry to say the wife died and the husband . . ."

"Wait. She *died!?* Are you sure?"

"Yes mam. The husband is in bad shape. No one here knows what's to be done with the kids."

"You don't worry about the kids. We'll take care of that. We'll be there shortly."

The accent had been unmistakably Vietnamese, yet he never introduced himself and, to this day I have no idea who made that phone call or how he knew to call us at all. But the fact that he did meant that we got to the hospital soon enough to intervene with the placement of the kids. An occurrence which would have long reaching ramifications and one for which I will be forever grateful to this caring caller, this earth angel.

In a hurried daze, I went into our bedroom and tapped Wayne's shoulder. He opened his eyes and looked up at me, immediately aware that something was wrong.

"Ha and Phat have been in an accident." He was still groggy but his eyes were riveted on me. "Wayne, she's dead."

He looked at me incredulously, "Dead?"

"Yes, and we have to get down there before someone gets to the kids."

"Should we wake Tim?"

"He'll be asleep for hours, I think we can get there and back before he wakes up."

The phone rang again and I went to answer it as Wayne hurried to get dressed.

"Miss Terri?" It was Oanh's serious voice coming over the line, in an unusual quaver.

Oanh is the oldest girl. Six years younger than Tim and the first in the subsequent stair-step of siblings, she's the one who at nine years old was left in charge when Tim exited the family. Serious and watchful, she had been left with responsibilities too wide for her narrow, young shoulders. She managed to change diapers, cook meals, mend clothes, learn bus schedules, translate for her parents, ready kids for school and make the honor roll all at the same time. She was always moving fast, her young lips pressed in a tight line, rarely smiling, always thinking ahead to the next possible crisis.

"Hey sweetie," I offered not knowing how much she knew.

"I got a call from the hospital. My mom's been in an accident and I don't know what to do." Her manner was firm and direct.

"I know, sugar, they called here too. Is anyone there with y'all?"

"No mam. It's just us."

"Okay, well look, you don't worry about anything. We're going down to the hospital and find out what's happened but first we'll stop by and check on y'all okay? Have y'all had breakfast?"

"We're doing that now."

"Okay, well you get the kids fed and we'll be there in a few minutes." Before I could say "good-bye," she hung up.

Click. She had her marching orders and she was on it.

We hadn't really needed to stop by but the hospital was only minutes from their house and I wanted to make sure they were all there and accounted for. The smell of fried egg lingered as we stepped into the large living room of the old sagging house. They were so glad to see us. Their relief was evident as they ran to us and hugged our legs and waists screeching a barrage of questions. "Where's our mom?" "Did she hit her head?" "Is it bad?" "Will she have to have an operation"? "When will she be able to come home?"

To say it was a heart wrenching scene doesn't even touch it. It took all the strength I had not to break down in sobs right there in front of them. But, we had to get to the hospital to verify our information before moving forward.

"Listen," I said to them as I gathered them around me, "I think y'all are going to be coming to stay with us for a few days so what I need for you to do is to each pack your backpack, and then after everyone is packed up, go ahead and give the house a good cleaning." I was desperate to keep them busy. I just could not stand for them to be so worried and fretful.

At the hospital we found their mother's pastor, a social worker, and several people from Catholic Community Services where the family had gotten English lessons and much needed aid and friendship. They, as well as the hospital staff, were obviously stricken and told us that while the mother was in fact dead, the father languished in ICU with severe injuries.

"Who will take six children?" old Pastor Phuong lamented.

"It'd be just plain cruel to split them up now," the social worker countered.

This line of thinking struck me as completely strange, almost idiotic. This waiting room was full of competent and caring professionals, all at a complete loss as to what to do with the children. Did they not know that we'd take responsibility for them? Did they think that we'd let them grieve with strangers? I spoke up, "We'll take the kids home with us." I didn't even have to look at Wayne; I knew he was thinking the exact thing. And, although the tension remained thick, there was a collective sigh, and even some tears, of relief.

What I remember most is the morning after. I opened the door of our spare bedroom, a room that typically held only the stark ironing board and cold iron. On this day, however, a lone stream of soft sunlight fell on a jumble of taut little legs and arms. Tousled black heads stuck out randomly from beneath the worn, brown security blanket one of them had doggedly dragged over the tragic day before. The slumbering huddle had abandoned a recent wet spot on the carpet, apparently scooting en masse, and were finally all deeply asleep. The baby's bottle lay abandoned and half-empty.

Before leaving for work, I had peeked in to see if anyone was awake after the long night of rocking and sobbing. Wayne had spent most of the time in the rocking chair in his study and, when I wasn't lying with them, I had spent the night shuttling kids, one at a time, to his lap to be rocked and soothed back to sleep. Wayne's sonorous tenor voice wafted softly through the darkness, beginning what would become a nightly ritual of singing them to sleep.

As a young girl, I had claimed that Jesus was the anchor of my heart, even sang about it clapping and swaying in the comfort of the congregation. But on this morning my heart was a sore, red mass bobbing at sea, not knowing how, not knowing what, not even knowing the right questions to ask as my restless eyes fell on little Quy whose birthday had been the day before. Their mom had planned to take them all to the amusement park that evening after work, a huge event for which she had scraped together her hard-earned pennies. I stared at the sweet face of the boy who was always running and smiling, remembering how Wayne had dashed out to buy a grocery store cake and presents after he'd learned about the birthday plans gone awry. I hadn't been so sure but he insisted that "this boy was not going to lose his sixth birthday along with everything else" and argued that a "party" may offer them at least a brief reprieve. He was right. Their excitement could not be contained as they sang "Happy Birthday" and excitedly watched Quy unwrap a heap of plastic toys. Cake and ice cream was not their general fare and they were delighted if only for a brief 30 minutes.

As I stood that morning staring into the quiet room, my heart was heavy; to be honest it was sinking. Not only with the sadness of their situation but also with the weight of uncertainty. And, that's when I heard it. My reminiscence was interrupted by a voice in my head that took me by complete shock. I actually *heard* Robin Williams roaring, "Gooooood Morning Vietnaaam!!!!!" And I smiled, in spite of myself, at the huddled mass before me. I smiled a real smile and for the first time in at least a day, my heart unclenched. I instinctively knew that God had a sense of humor and more importantly, a plan. I was able to take a full breath and go to work having no answers but knowing that it would be more than good.

Given what lay ahead, that feeling of peaceful assurance would, more often than not, leave me in the following days, months, years, but I never forgot that moment and often thought back to it for strength.

In the ensuing chapters, I will share with you the tools, strategies, truths, which were shared with me after I became the mother of six neglected, abused, traumatized, grief-stricken, beautiful, glorious children, overnight. At the time, I was young and energetic and well intentioned. I had a big heart but a limited skill set when it came to parenting.

The kids, three boys: Tim, Quy and John (18, 6, 2) and three girls: Oanh, Gabbie and Chau (11, 10, 8) had just lost their mother who was the only slight sense of security in their perpetually unstable world. The injuries sustained by their father also claimed his life two weeks later. But, wait, there's more.

It was two weeks before school started, our house was too small, the baby didn't speak English and had never been apart from an immediate family member in all of his life. As a group they shared a history of neglect, abuse, estrangement, abandonment, and trauma that was now compounded by a consuming grief and the fear that they'd be separated. There were school supplies and clothing to be procured, a move to a bigger house, heart-wrenching funerals to attend, lawyers and cloying, estranged relatives to deal with, not to mention the vast dental needs! Two of them were in the same grade, three were in the wrong grade, one needed to be potty-trained and while they shared a strong familial allegiance, there were bitter resentments at varying levels and intensities among them.

Three years later, after the initial and considerable dust settled in the form of legal adoption, after a few very costly grade skips, after three dogs, two birds, three sets of braces and Tim's graduation from high school, after several lost teeth and myriad homemade birthday cakes and neighborhood parties, we relocated. Wayne accepted a position at a university in Oregon. So we "loaded up the truck and we moved to Beverly." More like a converter van towing our car and in Quy's words, the "giantest U-Tauh truck they make!" The trip was boisterous, the move drastic, and yet just as refreshing and right as that of the Clampett's.

Okay. Admittedly, most of you did not start out with the Asian version of the Brady Bunch (sans Alice who, I might add, was sorely missed). I realize that you did not begin your foray into parenting with a guaranteed minimum wash load of 84 socks per week. But, we do have one thing in common which I suspect is true for most people: parenting offers the opportunity for personal expansion like few other life experiences. Nothing grew me more effectively than trying to be a good parent; I believe this is true for many people. The realization that those you love most, especially in the adolescent years, are beyond your control comes in many forms and stages. Sometimes it comes when the kids are 2, sometimes at 22.

This realization, for me, came incrementally through years of grappling with mystifying and obstinate behaviors, mean faces, snide remarks (and I wish I were talking about the kids here). It came through a shocking degree of anger, emotional isolation, and very scary close calls that led to desperation, which led to help. I should mention here that I had a propensity for denial so strong that, if bottled by the Pentagon as a defense mechanism, it would have assured our nation's safety forever! What took me years to learn and then unlearn and then relearn will not take as long for those more sensitive, open minded and honest about their feelings from the start.

These tools were procured throughout my initial catapult into parenthood and my subsequent career in teaching when I began facilitating parenting workshops for the school district in which I taught. I was asked to teach them because the material I had been assimilating since graduate school, coupled with professional training and mentoring I had received, had borne significant fruit in the classroom. These workshops led to work with parents of truant teenagers and then to working with private clients.

Yet, I was loath to bring my own personal journey into what I did professionally. I was still at a place in my life where, fostered by my culture, I tended to focus on all the mistakes (so many!) I'd made with my own kids instead of what I'd learned through and with them, and they through me.

After all, I had plenty of research to bear out my points, both of the "literature" and action research from my own classroom experience as well as the experiences of parents and other teachers who employed these methods. What good would telling *my* story do? I could not see how the natural, organic experiences of my life (both good and bad) created the very basis of strength on which I stood. My perception was that my kids made me look better than I really was.

After I'd gained some significant insight into my own learned ability to mistrust the past, present and especially the future, I became appreciative of the totality of my experience as a person and as a parent. Mostly, I gained enough distance to see the differing outcomes between my early parenting skills (or lack thereof) and those I eventually acquired. Because we learn as we go, I see that my younger kids had a much more satisfying time of it than the older ones.

I also began to forgive myself, to see myself in the light of my own life and to see that my parenting story could be helpful to others who are in the midst of similar struggles. So, I share this now with you because as the poet and author Maya Angelou so aptly and simply admonishes, "If you get, GIVE. If you learn, TEACH."

Let's Start at the Very Beginning

One day early on in my career, I sat at my supervisor's desk complaining. I was dealing with troubled kids and their often disengaged families and it was "so harrrrrd!" I just didn't know what to do in one situation or another. My supervisor, Joyce Saul, the grey-haired, twinkle-eyed pragmatist, clasped her hands firmly on the desk and leaned toward me. Her question came in her outspoken, favorite aunt kind of way, "What is it that you want?"

"I want to stay until 5:00 to have a parent conference."

"We close at 4:00."

"I know, but the parent works and it's difficult for her to get off early."

"Does she have a lunch break?"

"Yes."

"So, do you plan to take more responsibility for her child's education than she does? Can that really be helpful to them in the long run?"

"Well, I . . ."

"And, how long will you continue this trend?"

"I'm not sure . . ."

"Will you be in this student's life longer than his mom will?"

"Of course not, but . . ."

"Didn't you tell me that you love the time spent with your own kids when you all get home at the end of the day? Who will be with them while you're here?"

"Yes, hmm . . ."

"We close at 4:00. We don't pay the campus monitors to stay and the school secretary is gone for the day. We go home because this is a wonderful, rewarding job that allows us to be creative in solving problems. It is not our life."

I remember this moment vividly because her advice went up against my basic world-view: I was to sacrifice myself, both at work and at home, in order to help others. I came to her desk looking for sympathy, but I got my professional compass reset instead. And, as it turned out, I was able to come up with a solution that met the needs of the parent and the teacher.

I came to learn that Joyce's initial response to any teacher, student, or parent who presented themselves at her desk was to firmly ask, "What is it that you want?" This question makes so much sense. When we find ourselves with a seeming problem, we are obviously not getting what we desire. So, at the outset, isn't it clarifying for all parties involved to go ahead and state clearly what you'd like as a possible outcome?

It's what Maria taught the Von Trapp children in *The Sound of Music.* "Let's start at the very beginning. A very good place to start. When you read you begin with A-B-C. When you sing you begin with do-re-mi." You start with the basics and you build from there. Once we establish what it is we want, whether it's to sing or to sanely maintain a busy household or classroom, the outcome comes into focus.

This question, asked in earnest, became the foundation for all of my discussion with anyone in a perceived state of roadblock. I suggest they write it on the bedroom mirror, tuck it into the car's sun visor, tape it to the dashboard or bicycle handlebars. Put it on the refrigerator, above the washer and dryer, anyplace eyes regularly land. Through this book, we'll soon see that if the answer to this question that you ask yourself has to do with changing anyone else's behavior besides your own, then you can go back to "do" and realize the implausibility of this. This will enable you to take a look at your own attitudes and possible courses of action in moving forward.

A Pebble in a Pond

Long before I arrived on the teaching scene, Joyce, along with artist and teacher Gloria McRae, founded a program on behalf of the school district's need for expulsion placements. For many years, these two women worked alongside district staff, teachers, workshop facilitators, as well as with parole officers, judges, and law enforcement officers in honing a safe place where "unconditional, positive, regard" was the expectation for and from everyone in the building.

They built and established a very successful curriculum based on owning personal responsibility called *Social Survival Skills*. I taught teenagers in this program, eventually implementing my own research on the Adolescent Life Stage, which was built chiefly on the work of Erik Erikson (1902-1994).

Erikson was a psychologist who postulated that the modern human lifespan, from infancy to late adulthood, could be divided into 8 Psychosocial Stages of Development. I know, kind of a mouthful, huh? But, it's really quite simple. Broken down, "psycho" refers to the mind while "social" refers to the people around us. Basically, *our development is directly affected by the significant people in our lives*. The way we think and feel about ourselves and the world around us is largely dependent on those who take care of us or who live with us day to day.

Erikson purports that there is a conflict to be resolved in each of these stages. He calls these "crises" meaning decision point. We begin making decisions toward a healthy or unhealthy view of life very early on, like baby-early. Amazing, right? Based on the graphic you can see that the stages work in ripple effect.

Erikson's Eight Developmental Stages

The outcome of the first stage has a constant effect on the ultimate outcome of the others, just like throwing a pebble into a pond. The child's development, as well as the adult's is dependent on their previous outcomes (the way they presently think and feel) and on who is in their lives at present. The person or persons who create our social environment will dictate, to a great extent, the resolution of conflict in the present stage as well as influencing our next stage of development.

For example, in the Infancy Stage (1), dependence is on a primary caregiver. In the Toddler Stage (2), the circle broadens to other family members or perhaps daycare providers. The Early Childhood Stage (3) brings even more people into our lives in the form of teachers, bus drivers, lunchroom workers, crossing guards, etc. All of these affect our world.

You can see that each stage brings a broadening of community. In other words, as we get bigger, our world gets bigger as well. The way we choose to interact with our current world is a result of perceptions that begin very early on. The best part about all of this, for our purposes, is the Adolescent Stage (5). This is where, if the previous stages have not been so great, we can begin to turn the ship around for ourselves as well as our children. As you will later see, it is the point of power.

Casting Off Martyrdom

The students I taught had been given few if any choices about their lives and believed themselves to be victims of their parents, their friends, society, and especially of a school system that had "kicked them out." Some of them really had been victims early on and continued this trend by acting as if they still had no power even though they were now clearly making decisions that affected their home life and their schooling. In their own minds, there was a clear and evident disconnection between their actions and the outcomes of those actions. As far as I could see, they were in the perfect developmental stage to begin to transcend the victimization of their childhood. So, I began to give them choices right away. And because *I* was learning not to be a martyr myself, they were choices that worked both for me and for them.

For example, students were not allowed in classrooms until class started. Neither were they allowed to congregate outside the building. Therefore, they all arrived en masse as the doors were opened each morning. One year, I had a student arrive 30 minutes early each day due to her dad's work schedule. Unlike many of our students, she did not like hanging out at the municipal bus mall downtown with the other kids. She waited alone outside my classroom no matter what the weather.

I offered her the opportunity to come inside in exchange for wiping desks and tabletops while I continued to prep for my day. Eventually, some of the other early arrivals asked to come in and I agreed, in exchange for tasks that I needed to get done, like reworking the bulletin board or posting the day's schedule.

I was delighted at the response to this. I saw that these kids lapped up being needed like a kitten laps up milk. Due to their parents' socio-economic status, and/or due to their own behaviors, many of them had been "cases" for most, if not all of their lives. Not much had been expected of them so they did not feel they had much to offer.

Over time, I started each new school year by allowing the students to help put the room together. This meant that I could then use the days before students arrived each year to work on curriculum and attend requisite staff meetings without shouldering the gargantuan task of organizing the classroom all by myself. It also allowed for some major student buy-in to the atmosphere as we set up areas assigned for different uses such as reading, computer work, studying, recycling, etc. My students and I created the culture of our classroom pertinent to the year ahead. They were able to contribute in a very real and much appreciated way while I was able to cast off some of the self-imposed martyrdom of being a teacher with too much to do and never enough time to do it.

This sense of community and culture was especially helpful because expulsions happen sporadically. Our district was a large one, encompassing the capital city and more, so there were new students entering the classroom continually. The expectations were clear and my class expected incoming students to fall in line as well.

I had this point driven home to me one day as I stood in front of the classroom. As was our routine, I had personally checked in with each student as the others quietly wrote in their journals. The only light in the room was that of the overhead projector. I had long before eschewed more modern technology when I discovered the calming effect that the projector's fan, coupled with the lights being off, had on my classroom. The students sat quietly in the semi-lit room with little to compete with their thoughts. Late arrivers were greeted with whispers as if they were entering a quiet theater. After everyone was checked in, the lights came on and I welcomed the class as a group.

On this particular day, there was a new kid in the room. It was his first day. He was alluring in that bad boy sort of way. His faded black jeans, black leather jacket and white t-shirt were reminiscent of a teenage rebel of the 1950's but his hair was longer, slung over his eyes, and he had on the ever popular Doc Martens. He exuded aloof coolness and confidence and, of course, chose a seat next to Mandy, the prettiest girl in the room.

Mandy had been in my class the year prior. She had great buy-in, and had made remarkable gains both academically and socially. Coming from a background of addicted parents who were sometimes in jail, Mandy and her sister had ended up in foster care in years prior. She had endured horrific experiences and bore the tinges of Post Traumatic Stress Disorder that showed itself chiefly in the classroom as pronounced anxiety. She talked fast and often, and initially had trouble with conversational turn-taking. She was pleasant and liked to laugh but was also brutally honest with herself and others. At 16, she held a job, lived on her own, and managed to have a circle of supportive friends and family.

Early on and often, I explained to my students that I was a bit ADD (Attention Deficit Disorder) so if they talked while I was talking, I would stop and kindly let them finish their conversation so I wouldn't lose my train of thought. This truth was a great leveler in my classroom. Students usually self-monitored and helped monitor each other when I was addressing them.

On this particular morning, Mandy's intense blue eyes were on me. She and the other class members knew the drill. They knew that I had already graduated from high school and that our being together in the classroom was about them and their obvious desire to do the same. They knew this because I often reminded them that they did not "have" to do anything in my classroom. The door was not locked, they could leave anytime they liked. Their being in the building was about their own stated need and wish to obtain a diploma.

The new kid knew none of this. He came into the classroom with the common assumption among newcomers: that he was now going to the "bad kid school," expecting that his classmates shared the mutual and often expected disdain for teachers and other authority figures. He attempted to make his mark by showing complete disinterest in me and especially in what I was saying. He repeatedly tried to begin a conversation with Mandy while I was talking. Trying not be impolite, she answered him curtly with a "yes" or a "no," a nod, or a half-smile.

Finally, she couldn't take it anymore. She turned to him, her long blonde hair flying in the wake of her quick movement. With exasperation, she blurted, "Dude, she's ADD. Shut the @#&★ up." Then she quickly turned back to me with a bird-like nod, "go ahead."

It was all I could do to continue without doubling over with laughter. Not only was cool-guy not admired for being openly noncompliant, he was chiefly ignored and very unexpectedly disciplined by a peer. He didn't appear embarrassed because no one was focusing on him but he did look noticeably uncomfortable as he took a quiet look around to realize that he was the only one not paying attention. I later thanked Mandy privately for trying to help and we were able to have a brief discussion about school appropriate language.

In truth, I was touched by Mandy's display of loyalty to the classroom standards as well as to her own priorities. I was astounded to see that I was teaching in the exact way I'd dreamed and was grateful to have gained the information and tools that led to such healthy relationships with most of my students and with my own children. Eventually, even cool-guy was no exception.

Bottom Line

Healthy relationships are built on a healthy relationship with ourselves. No more doormat, no more martyr, no more giving and giving and giving to depletion. No more attempts to control, no more resentments, no more guilt. Sigh a big sigh of relief. It's over. Any relationship you have from now on, be it with the man on the street or with a family member, must be equal in value to both of you. Therefore, you may ask yourself when approaching any person in order to "help" them, "What is it that *I* want from this?" As Maria Von Trapp would sing, "it'll bring you back to do."

Ask Yourself

Now is a good time to ask yourself what you want from this book. Why do you have it in your hands? What did you hope to gain by picking it up?

Try This

Jot down what your current relationship with your child is like. Then, write what you want. How would you like to see it evolve for you? For your child?

TAKE A BATH!

SECTION 1

The Life Stages

*What is necessary to change a person
is his awareness of himself."*

Abraham Maslow

Stage 1—The Infancy Stage: Trust vs. Mistrust

The Dumbest Person on the Smart Side of the Room

When I was in first grade, there was not as much thought given to self-esteem as there is today. Everything was based on academic marks and it was believed that if you learned enough reading and writing and arithmetic, you'd be successful in school and, ultimately, in life. I had no idea what school was about. I just knew I showed up and got to read and play and color. Having been too sickly and frail for kindergarten, first grade was my initial encounter with a class full of other children. I loved school, I loved learning, and I was eager and excited.

That's why my mother was puzzled when one fall day, I came home dejectedly dragging my new rubber-coated plaid book sack, rather than carefully carrying it and skipping onto the porch as I usually did. There was no boisterous slam of the screen door that day. I appeared in the kitchen quiet and somber.

Having a penchant for the dramatic, I sighed heavily and slumped in a chair at the kitchen table. Mama turned from stirring the red beans and creased her brow. "What's the matter with you? Better be careful or you're gonna trip over that bottom lip."

I lay my head in my arms and with one eye on her, mumbled into the tabletop, "I'm the dumbest person on the smart side of the room."

"I can't hear you when you talk into the table, Terri Adele." She glanced over at the washing machine that had just stopped spinning. Eager to get on to her next chore, she was impatient with me. "Pick your head up and tell me what's wrong."

Hearing my "in trouble" name, I flung myself into the back of the chair and just went ahead and told her the whole story. "We took a test today and I had to move desks because I got put on the smart side of the room."

"Well, that sounds like a good thing to me." She lit the burner under the rice and stuck her fists onto the waistband of her pedal pushers waiting for an explanation.

My voice quavered and my eyes pooled. "But I'm the dumbest kid on the smart side of the room."

To my utter surprise Mama dropped her head and chuckled as she made her way to the washer. Then, she started cracking up as she pulled the sodden clothes into the laundry basket. "You are something else again," she said as the screen door slammed behind her on her way to the clothesline.

I knew that was a compliment but I honestly had no idea what I had done to deserve it.

Mama relayed that story to my older siblings, the neighbors, my aunts and uncles and my grandparents. Everybody got a good laugh out of it but no one ever told me why it was funny; they assumed I knew. But I did *not* realize that I really was a smart kid. I did *not* know that I was one of the smartest kids on the smart side of the room. I thought the teacher had made a terrible mistake. I always assumed that most people knew more than I did. The tapestry of my 6-year-old life, like yours, had its beginnings in the early threads of self-perception, threads that begin in infancy. Threads that are pulled and woven by those significant others in our lives.

Our life stages from infancy to death give us the opportunity to choose between the positive and negative. In each developmental stage, we make a decision somewhere on the continuum between these two poles and move forward in that mode of inner belief about ourselves.

You can see from the following diagram that very early on, we are deciding if the world is a safe place or not. We are deciding if people are to be trusted. The basis for this decision is simple: are we or are we not being fed and cared for?

The way in which we answer this question in our little hearts, determines how we will proceed into our next developmental stage. Our care, or lack of care, determines our ability to trust or not to trust.

Infants do not have words; they have no language with which to speak to themselves or others. Theirs is a deeply felt, non-verbal knowing. I use a DVD clip in workshops that demonstrates this point beautifully. A young mother interacts with her baby and the child responds demonstratively pointing and smiling and gurgling. After a while the mother no longer responds and holds her face in a zombie-like stare. The child still tries to interact and when this proves futile the baby becomes upset, afraid, confused.

Healthy development during this stage is vital. Developmental lack can have serious and long-lasting effects. For instance, it is believed that the rare neurological condition, prosopagnosia (face-blindness) can be caused by a parent (significant other) who does not make eye contact with their baby during the infant stage. This disorder has no known cure and will be with a person for their lifetime.

The infant who is fed, held and tended to will move from the Infant Stage with an innate trust for other humans intact. Conversely, the infant who is not fed in a timely manner, not held, or not otherwise tended to will move from the Infant Stage with an innate mistrust in humans.

Stage 1 - Infancy		
"Can I trust, or not?"	Infant Stage (Birth-2)	Trust vs. Mistrust (Hope) Does the child believe its primary caregiver to be reliable? Is the child cared for on a consistent basis and not neglected? In other words, is the world to be trusted? Will I be cared for?

In my initial naivete as a parent, I figured on having my kids all patched up in time for college, secretly hoping to wave them off with a relieved sigh and a pat on my own back. I was so busy trying to run a household that I often (usually) overlooked the emotional havoc of school, friends, and crushes, in favor of clear lines. Imagine my surprise when I very quickly realized that my best laid plans didn't match up with reality. The kids just weren't cooperating with my great ideas and intentions. It wasn't that they were hellions or anything like that. It's just that I was unable to figure out what to do when problems or behaviors reared up requiring more than I was capable of.

It wasn't long at all before the throes of adolescence were throwing me for a complete loop and, eventually into the depths of humility as I witnessed painful grappling on so many fronts. I tried to help but felt like one trying to play ice hockey in stilettos. I was obviously not fully equipped for the game. First, I wasn't able to comprehend their perceived situations and second, I just couldn't get out of my *own* way. Here I was again: the dumbest kid on the smart side of the room. Thus began a slow simmer of unarticulated alarm. Help came when I finally went back to school and was introduced to Erik Erikson and realized that I, myself, was reacting in unexamined manners built on self-perceptions that had their roots in infancy.

The simple realization that we are **all** in stages of development lifted a considerable weight off my shoulders. It eliminated the notion that I was "done" simply because I was an adult and a parent. I had subconsciously assumed that development sort of tapered off once I reached adulthood. I also adopted another unexamined supposition. I somehow picked up the notion that I should intuitively know my children's needs and innately have the wherewithal to meet such needs. I kind of thought that's what the work "parent" implied. I never thought of a parent as a sort of shepherd, watching over and guiding as they themselves grew. It was such a relief to see that I was actually on a continuum and did not need to know everything. I was still very much moving toward wholeness and self-awareness in my own right. I could then see my kids and I as partners, like Dorothy and her gang skipping along the yellow-brick road toward self-actualization. We were not equals in experience, wisdom or knowledge, but we were on the same developmental path. This was huge!

By looking at these stages, I immediately gained insight into why, although I was a smart kid and adult, I never saw myself in that light. I realized that my self-perception had colored every aspect of my life and my relationships, regardless of what was true or not true in reality.

From birth we are deciding things. Of course, we have no language at birth, no terms with which to think about these decisions, so we feel them. We have feelings from the very beginning. Language is not yet in place but our feelings are innate and provide the basis for our reactions and interactions. This is why being in touch with our true emotional responses to life is key to our happiness; it is the true us.

Obviously none of us gets through life without some misguidance and therefore some missteps in our development. After all, we were raised neither by angels nor by the devil's spawn but by humans who do the best they know how. The author and motivational speaker, Louise Hay, describes in her book, *You Can Heal Your Life*, how we come into the world as being in touch with who we are. We know when to seek attention for our physical as well as emotional needs. There is a sense of demanding presence about us that seems to say, "I am someone!" Sometimes these demands are met and sometimes they are not. However, take heart, any lack that we, or our children, have experienced in these stages of development can be overcome.

Stage 2—The Toddler Stage: Autonomy vs. Shame and Doubt

"Baby, Baby, You Set My Heart In Motion."

My granddaughter, Freya, is a dynamic two-year old who is recently recognizing her own autonomy. Lately, I've noticed that she answers most questions asked of her with a resounding, "Me!"

Freya and I were having a discussion about Dorothy, Tin Man, Lion, and Scarecrow, a quartet she has recently discovered and loves. I get a kick out of hearing her attempts at pronunciation, so expecting to hear cute takes on the names of the yellow-brick-roaders, I asked, "Freya, who went to see the Wizard?"

"Meeee!" She smiled proudly as she brushed her index finger against her chest as if strumming her heartstrings. And, I believe that she is doing just that. She is affirming her spot in the world. She is loud and proud.

Later, I talked with Freya and her two older brothers about how fun it was going to be when they came to my house for an Easter Egg Hunt.

"Freya, who's coming to MaMere's (their name for me) house on Easter?"

Expecting her to respond with her attempt at the newly learned "Easter Bunny," she exclaimed instead, "Meee!"

Whether the question is "Who's ready for dinner," or "Who's ready for school," the answer is always the same: "Meeeeee!"

Now that she's gotten the hang of "going potty," she responds to this question in the same manner. And she's so excited about exclaiming her presence, every time, without fail. She grins and looks at us as if to say, "aren't you so happy that I'm here?"

Erikson lays great importance on potty training as the chief determinant of a healthy outcome in the toddler stage. He found that those toddlers who were encouraged in this most important developmental step were far more likely to be confident in their autonomy as opposed to those who were derided or ridiculed or otherwise unsupported in their efforts.

Picture this scene: A toddler emerging from the bathroom having tried to potty on her own. One of her legs is properly in her Pull-up while she clutches the other side to herself with her hand to keep them from falling to the ground. The potty seat is a bit wet and there is toilet paper in the potty and also remnants of her first attempt at wiping on the bathroom floor.

Her mother, who's been busy in the kitchen, is surprised when her daughter approaches with a proud, "My go potty, mommy."

Mommy smiles and leads her back to the bathroom. She helps with the clean up of both the bathroom and the toddler all the while applauding her attempts. "You knew you had to go potty." "You knew right where the potty was." "You got the toilet paper off the roll." "You almost got your Pull-ups all the way on." "I am so proud of you." You get the idea.

Now, picture the same scene. Only this time, as the child approaches her mother, she is met with an angry look as mom slams the dishes in the sink, grabs the toddler by the arm and jerks her toward the bathroom. "How many times have I told you not to make a mess?" "Look at this mess." "You tell me when you have to go." "I am sick of cleaning up after you." "Do you want me to put you back in diapers like a baby?" Again, you get the idea and you can judge for yourself which reaction will lead to a better development of *Autonomy* (the ability to do things by themselves) as opposed to *Shame and Doubt* (being insecure and afraid to try). Efforts count for a lot at this stage.

Stage 2 - Toddler		
"Can I do it, or not?"	Toddler Stage (2-4)	Autonomy vs. Shame/Doubt (Will) The child is beginning to see his or her self as a separate individual from the primary caregiver and needs to be encouraged to explore while being protected. "Can I do it?"

In the Toddler Stage, children are just beginning to realize that they are a separate being from their primary caretaker. During infancy, they are very much attached to another person. They are physically carried places whether they want to go or not. They are completely dependent on another human for their existence. Think about it. Early on, infants cannot even hold a bottle or a cracker. Now, in the toddler stage, they can feed themselves, drink from a cup, use utensils, go from one room to the next unaccompanied. Their newfound freedom is exhilarating for them but can be a little tricky (or "trixy" as my three-year old grandson says) for the parents. Thus, the "terrible twos" ensue. I'm here to tell you that they do not have to be terrible! They'll be busy, but not necessarily terrible.

Toddlers love trying new things. They are unshackled, unchained, they can walk, they can run, they can grab things! They are down low and can see their world (usually your house) from a very different perspective now. This freedom is akin to the zeal of a teenager who just got his driver's license. Wide open roads, baby!

Yet, someone is still trying to take them by the hand all the time. Harsh their mellow. Ruin their buzz. Thus we hear the word "no" quite often and quite vehemently. To us it seems defiant. To them, they are trying on autonomy to see how it fits, asking for room to be their own person, allowing you the opportunity to begin to recognize them in this new state.

This is where questions, as brilliantly suggested by the behavior management gurus at *Love and Logic®* become imperative for a healthy launch from this stage to the next. Also, questions can keep both parents and toddlers sane throughout because you are giving them what they intuitively know they need: a little choice in the matter of their own lives.

And, ultimately, isn't this what you want for your child? Or do you want a child who needs to be told what to do all the time by their friends, their boss, a spouse or partner? "Nuff said."

So, offer them low-cost choices that you can live with such as mittens or gloves, juice or milk, walking or being carried to bed, story or no story, water or no water, etc. This way, you are helping them think for themselves (*the* crucial skill in life) while keeping them safe and secure at the same time.

Ask questions. Ask them a lot. Be proactive as when approaching a crosswalk, for example. The question is not "do you want to hold daddy's hand?" which could lead to a big, fat, "NO!" The question is, "do you want daddy to hold your right hand or your left hand?" And ask at eye level when you can. Think of it as doing squats all day which will cut down your time at the gym!

Stage 3—Early Childhood: Initiative vs. Guilt

"Oh No! Silver!"

It was the last day before Christmas break, a really busy one in our first grade classroom. Mrs. Effler ran to and fro helping us get our work done before the end of the day. She allowed those who finished early the privilege of coloring the gigantic picture of Santa being pulled in his sleigh by the reindeer. The picture was spectacular; it was a coloring sheet that covered our whole bulletin board.

Of course, Leslie Davis was the first to be finished with her work. She was always the first to be finished with everything and she somehow seemed to know all the answers all the time. Whether in the classroom, the lunchroom, the library, or on the playground, Leslie was always there to inform us (as well as the teacher) if we did something wrong. She was tall and confident and I obeyed her implicitly.

Having finished my work early on, I wasn't far behind Leslie to the bulletin board and was happily coloring away with the others when my reverie was interrupted by Leslie's loud cry, "Mrs. Effler! Terri is coloring Santa's reins silver and she's ruining the whole picture!" Everyone stopped. I was mortified as all eyes turned toward the inappropriately shiny reins.

Mrs. Effler, busy helping the laggers, did not even look at the board but straight at me. Her usually sweet voice was stern. "Terri, sit down."

Then she turned back to her work as Leslie began a heroic attempt to cover over my mistake with a dark brown crayon.

I slinked off to my desk to hide my head in my arms.

It wasn't until I was 40 years old that I realized the proper color for Santa's reins *was* silver! Silver. The color of ice and frost and fairy dust. The color that represents the shiny magic of Christmas more than any other. Not rope *brown*. Santa's not a freakin' farmer! He's *Santa*!

Had I developed a healthy sense of myself like Leslie, I may have made this case right then and there, but the thought never occurred to me. My automatic assumption was that she was right and I was wrong. Period.

Leslie and I had developed on opposite sides of Erikson's developmental crises resulting in her having a very healthy self-esteem and in my not. As an adult, this revelation caused me to do some soul searching which led to an ongoing rediscovery of myself and of my talents and abilities. I became a healthier person, which means that I became a healthier parent, as well as a healthier teacher.

In Stage 3, we are deciding if we should take initiative or if we just don't know any better and should then not try at all. According to Erikson, who coined the term "identity crisis," we are all, from birth to death, coming to grips with ourselves in relation to the world around us. The word "crisis" actually means a time for decision and not some horrible event, which is how we've come to use the word. Times of crisis call for a decision as in the case of a heart attack where you may have to *decide* between doing CPR or calling an ambulance. The crisis is not the event, but the decision involved around the event.

Even though they are very young, children in this stage of development have already had a lot of input regarding their ability to do well or not in their attempts. This is why our words are so important at this stage as we endeavor to help the little ones make steps forward into self-realization.

Stage 3 – Early Childhood		
"Is it safe to try something new, or not?"	Early Childhood Stage or PreSchool (4-7)	Initiative vs. Guilt (Purpose) Does the child have the ability to do things or is the child made to feel guilty about making his or her own choices?

Scenario: 2 first-graders sitting side by side at the art table. Child #1 has a very healthy sense of self and due to positive input during the previous stages of life, is buoyantly confident. Child #2 has a sense of self that leans to the opposite side. They both have the exact picture and are busily coloring. There is no visible difference between levels of ability.

As the teacher walks by she attempts to encourage the children: "These pictures look so nice. You've only gone out of the lines a few times!"

Child #1 zeros in on the first part of the comment: "These pictures look so nice." The child smiles and continues coloring happily.

Child #2 focuses on the second part of the comment and basically hears, "you've gone out of the lines." He slams his crayon on the table in front of him, folds his arms across his chest and hangs his head.

From this example you can see that, even though they are in the same exact situation, they have differing reactions based on their already established predispositions.

The same is true for us at each level of development. We are in "crisis" at each stage. Successful resolution of each conflict in our current stage of development will result in a favorable outcome that allows us to enter more healthily into the following stage of development. Each stage allows for self-awareness and identity, which ultimately affect meaning and purpose.

Stage 4—Later Childhood: Industry vs. Inferiority

The Gospel According to Saul

One of my life-changing mentors was my school supervisor, Joyce Saul. She is one of the most loving and down-to-earth people I've ever met. Joyce's no-nonsense manner regarding children has been sought out by many. Throughout our tenure together, I had opportunities to hear about and to be profoundly affected by Joyce's particular style of parenting and living. She always said, "*Your* life and *your* family take precedent over everything else you do."

Case in point: once her 2 sons were old enough to understand the concept of money, she and her husband sat them down each year and told them how much money she earned teaching, and how much their dad earned through his dental practice. They then laid out all the family and household expenses.

"This is how much it costs to maintain the house and yard. I enjoy living here, as you do, but I'd be okay living someplace cheaper like a 2-bedroom apartment as long as it had a washer and dryer."

Thus began the discussion of the cost of maintenance as opposed to salary. The boys really enjoyed having separate rooms. They liked having the yard and liked having space to have their friends over. It was obvious, what with the mortgage and cost of living, they could not afford to pay extra for the required upkeep of the place. Each year the group decided to get the house and yard maintenance done on Saturday mornings. Four people working for two hours equaled eight hours of labor. This was a mutual agreement satisfactory to all parties; it was not a cute exercise.

Joyce led a full life and had commitments outside the home that were important to her. She was dedicated to her school staff and students; she was committed to her church and surrounding activities. She was extremely involved in the lives of her aging parents and devoted to the education of her sons, one of whom had a profound learning disability. She did not intend to be swallowed up with overwhelming chores. And, she really was okay living in an apartment if that's what it took.

Each year, these boys were offered a very important place in the life of their family. They were able to contribute to their own wellbeing and that of their parents, in an age appropriate manner and within their means. They were moving, in concrete steps, from childhood to adulthood because they were aware that what they contributed mattered, and made a difference in the comfort of their home.

Their self-esteem was boosted. They saw themselves as important and worthy, as capable and smart. This happened within themselves and therefore translated over into all that they did, producing a healthy impact at school as well.

In other words, these boys had no problem trying what interested them whether it was an entry in the Science Fair or choir or football. They were not afraid to try.

Stage 4 – Later Childhood		
"Am I good enough, or not?"	Later Childhood Stage or School Age (6-11)	Industry vs. Inferiority (Competence) The child compares self-worth to others (such as in a classroom environment) and can recognize major disparities relative to other children.

By Stage 4, we have a pretty good sense of whether we can accomplish what we try successfully or not based on our experiences in the previous stages. Therefore, we have an innate sense about trusting ourselves and our abilities thus far.

Kids in this stage run the gamut between those at school who will try out for choir, sports, band, enter the science fair, or volunteer (industrious) and those who are afraid to do these things (inferior). I've had many discussions with high school students who can look back on their own lives and totally relate. Some said they ended up hanging out with the "bad" kids because they didn't have to do anything to fit in. They did not need to succeed at anything. In retrospect, they can see that these were ideas they had about themselves which they rarely if ever verbalized. Some say that they can see it now and wish they would've known about these stages much earlier.

Stage 5—The Adolescent Stage: Identity vs. Identity Confusion

Love and Potato Salad

My sixth grade teacher wrote me a poem once. It was a funny little rhyme about how my stomach was in danger of popping. One of my classmates delivered this poem to me as I lay in the sick room behind the principal's office after lunch. Our lunches were always fabulously home-cooked meals. On this day we had been served some of my favorites: roast, rice and gravy, yeast rolls and potato salad. I could not understand how so many of my classmates could leave the scoop of yellow deliciousness sitting on their plates. So, after I finished mine, I ate six more helpings. Apparently, my eyes were bigger than my stomach so my teacher (an all time favorite of mine) good-naturedly excused me from the first 15 minutes of class and sent me with a note to the sick room.

Mama always made potato salad when we went on outings involving extended family and swimming. These times with my beloved cousins and water, which is still my favorite mode of play, were as precious as Christmas morning to me. All of our cares were forgotten, my siblings didn't fuss or fight, and

Mama was laughing and smiling. She loved being with her parents, aunts, uncles, brothers and sisters and their families. Her joy was palpable, which by the time I got to adolescence, was a rare occurrence indeed.

I gained a fair amount of weight in the sixth grade. There were certain things that I just could not pass up. It wasn't until I was an adult that I associated my obsession with certain foods with emotional eating. Looking back, I saw that this was an especially rocky time in my young life. Yet, due to my usual tolerant manner, that fact never entered my consciousness. Home was home. My family was my family. There were some tense moments. There were some happy times. That was that.

Except for knowing how to feel hurt, sad, happy or excited, I was pretty checked out emotionally. Food helped in this way. Feelings that I could not identify were easy to press down with a few helpings of anything. And sugar really took the edge off of anxiousness. Still does.

I stuck my finger down my throat at my cousin's rehearsal dinner. I was 12 at the time. My sister and I were at a steak place, around a happy table with my girl cousins and our fun aunts. We were having such a great time; I did not want it to end but I was so full of the delicious steak that I couldn't take another bite. So, I relieved my stomach and went back to the table to finish my dinner. I had never done that before and I have not done it since but it could have been detrimental and it was obviously not normal behavior. Again, this never occurred to me.

My compulsive behavior around food was firmly entrenched by this time. Because I was so physically active during high school, I wasn't overweight. Even though my dress size was 3, diets were always alluring and I never would have counted myself as physically attractive. Emphasis in my family was placed on being attractive more than being smart. We were judged constantly and often harshly. Of course, in the Southern way, it was never mean, "You know that cake you're eating is fattening, right?" Just mentioned as encouragement, just trying to "help."

This is only one of the issues that I tugged along with me through life as part of my identity. Once I exited my adolescent phase, loving food and not being thin enough were part of my self-perception. I remember being at a wedding when I was 21. I marveled at the sister of the bride who was so happily intent on getting pictures with her camera while a pile of chicken-salad sandwiches sat right there at her finger tips! How could she think of anything else?

Food issues and body image were just a couple of the major issues that clouded my perception of myself and the world around me. Yet I never questioned these until I was an adult. And herein lies the key: it's never too late to go back and resolve attitudes and actions that no longer serve us.

In my work, I focus particularly on the fifth stage of development: Adolescence. This seems to be where many of us lose our footing. Children in this stage often come into it unprepared for the inherent freedoms and life-altering choices they are faced with. They have not had much practice in personal responsibility having relied on parents to cook their meals, figure out their schedules, solve their problems for them and just otherwise think for them, in general. That's why some kids have a very difficult time here. They get taller but not necessarily more grown up.

As seen in the following diagram, adolescents are faced with the all-time important question of "who am I?" They have lots of input into their lives at this point from family, friends, school, the world at large. Most importantly, here is the chance for parents to allow exploration while helping to maintain safety. A sometimes difficult prospect indeed.

Stage 5 - Adolescence		
"Do I know who I am, or not?"	Adolescence (Puberty)	Identity vs. Identity Confusion (Fidelity) Questioning of self. Who am I? How do I fit in? Where am I going in life? Erikson believes that children allowed to explore and conclude their own identity will not face identity confusion. Those who are continually pushed to conform to another's views will face identity confusion.

Adolescence is also the stage that parents tend to fear most. They become afraid of becoming disconnected from their child, of losing control, and sometimes of losing touch with them altogether. So, they begin to tighten their grip when the direct opposite is what's required for healthy development.

What I do is help parents see that this stage is a chance to make up for any lost time in the previous stages. It truly is the stage, if handled rightly that can create a whole new world in the relationship of parent and child. It's a chance for parents to see very clearly that this child's life is his own, often a bitter pill to swallow on the outset. It is *the* most powerful stage of all because it can be the avenue through which teenagers recognize their abilities, their talents, and their predispositions. Knowing themselves then, they are able to increasingly manage relationships and conduct their lives in a fulfilling manner.

The adolescent stage is also particularly striking to me because, as Hans Sebald points out in his book, *Adolescence,* there is no clear marker in our culture from childhood to adulthood. Therefore, there is no clear passageway from one stage to the next. For instance, in some cultures, when a girl begins to menstruate she is accepted as a woman and given all of the responsibilities and duties thereof. Her way is made clear. She will have children and care for them and cook and garden.

In the same way, when a boy is able to prove himself in a culturally designated deed, he is considered to be a man. He is then expected to hunt and gather with the other men. This is his job, if you will. The movement from childhood to adulthood is crystal clear; there is no limbo. There is no guessing as to when a child should be allowed to take on adult responsibilities or what their job will be in society.

Obviously, this is not the case in our modern day society. Adolescence for us becomes a sort of artificial gap between childhood and adulthood, a gap widened, according to Sebald, by the advent of Industrialization.

Before this period in our history, vocation was hardly an issue. If your parents were teachers, you would likely become a teacher. If your parents were farmers, you would continue to work on the farm. If your parents were grocers, you would carry on the family business. Once machinery and factories came along, however, people poured into cities for jobs that had little to do with their families or upbringing. As it stands today, adolescents have myriad choices when it comes to job or career. Even if their parents own a business, they have the choice to do something totally different. This is a good thing and allows for flexibility and fluidity in life. But it does create yet another unclear path.

This is why the adolescent stage is emotionally painful and unnecessarily drawn out in our current culture. Johnny or Sally, depending on their bodies and social experiences, may begin this stage as early as 10. If their parents allow them to begin to think for themselves and to reason, to explore their capabilities and interests, they arrive on the other end of this stage with some significant personal insight. But if Sally and Johnny are given the privileges of adulthood without the personal accountability, they never find a true sense of who they are before they age out of the stage. Thus, they age without maturing. So, it's relatively easy to see why some of us miss this mark and then continue with a sort of fragmented limp into the rest of our lives.

When I began sharing this information with teenagers in my classroom, they were quite reasonably astounded: "I've been making decisions since birth? Why hasn't anyone ever told us this before?" Sometimes this was asked in bewilderment and sometimes in outrage. I don't know the answer to that question but for kids (as with adults) this information is really helpful to know and the earlier, the better.

Stage 6—Young Adulthood: Intimacy vs. Isolation

Happy If Only . . .

My inability to connect with my daughter first drove me to counseling initially for her but ultimately for myself. I was not able to control her behaviors or her attitudes with my cadre of threats and heartfelt concerns. She was wading into some deep water and I realized she could possibly drown. This scared me. Up until this point, I figured she'd age out of some of her propensities, especially the one where she just completely shut down and shut herself off from the family.

This was especially hurtful because of her wit and humor, her sensitivity and her ability to laugh so well. When she withdrew in anger she was sorely missed. She was having a really rough time and I did not know how to help her. So I took her to someone who I hoped could.

After a few sessions the counselor, a really nice woman, called me into her office to tell me that my daughter was not interested at all in getting better. "Basically, you're wasting her time and your money." I was shocked. I had never been to a counselor before. In my naivete, I assumed my daughter would be "fixed" in a few sessions and we'd be on our merry way.

The counselor shared with me her estimation that my daughter had a possible attachment disorder. She explained to me that this was a broad term used to describe people who were unable to attach emotionally. "It occurs often in children who have been separated from their caregivers at an early age or those who have been abused or neglected at an early age." I was heartbroken. This was a kid that I not only loved but enjoyed immensely. I wanted to be attached to her. I wanted her to be attached to me. "What about marriage?" I asked.

"She'll probably marry someone who is also emotionally unavailable. People do it all the time." She smiled kindly at me as my jaw dropped. Then, I got mad. Not only was this woman not helping, she was giving me some awful news that neither she nor I could fix. "That is *not* okay with me," I snapped at her like it was her fault. And then she said something that changed my life. She looked at me and calmly said, "Okay."

"Okay? What does that mean?!?"

"It means you can be 'not okay' with it but it won't change it."

I was taken aback. Totally at a loss. I had never had anyone suggest acceptance to me before. I was completely at sea and I knew it.

"Okay, then," I said to her. "If she doesn't want help then I need help in knowing how to live with her." And I proceeded to make my first ever counseling appointment.

I was greatly helped in these sessions both with my own unwillingness to be intimate and in understanding my daughter's inability to be intimate. I've since heard intimacy described as "into-me-see." In other words, when we are intimate with another person, we allow them to see who we really are, we don't cover up because we trust that they will accept us. As I tell my students, intimacy is not a synonym for sex although people use the words interchangeably. In fact, people have sex all the time with people they don't even know!

I could see that my daughter was not making the cross into the *Intimacy* side of Erikson's Stage 6 crisis. She was far more comfortable with *Isolation* stemming from her experiences in early childhood.

Stage 6 – Young Adulthood		
"Who will I love; what will I do?"	Young Adulthood (20-40)	Intimacy vs. Isolation (Love) Who do I want to be with? Will I settle down? What will I do with my life? This stage has begun to last longer as young adults choose to stay in school and not settle. Successfully forming loving relationships with other people allows for the experience of love and intimacy.

This is Erikson's point. Our development not only relies on our associations with other people but it also prepares us for future relationships. How we are treated determines how we respond. How we respond and ultimately navigate all of our relationships including those with work, and society as well as family, determines our happiness.

In 2009, *The Atlantic Magazine* ran an article by Joshua WolfShenk entitled, *What Makes Us Happy?* For 72 years Harvard researchers followed the lives of 268 men through college in the late 1930's, on into war, careers, marriages, divorce, illness, parenthood, loss of spouse, loss of child, financial ruin, financial success and ultimately into old age. And after 268 men, 72 years, and several teams of researchers, the findings boil down to this: "It is social aptitude not intellectual brilliance or parental social class that leads to successful aging."

In other words, it's our relationships that ultimately define our happiness.

I hear people say all the time that they'd be happy "if only." And you could fill that lonely "only" spot with a million things: more money, better kids, a different job, no job, a better partner, no partner, better looks, etc. Any book we read or thing we do or stuff we take or people we love—basically any pursuit—is taken with the hope of making us happy, right? You, yourself, are probably reading this book with the hope of making your life happier. But, when you think about it, what really makes us successful in life is not how smart or beautiful or gifted we are. Ultimately, if we cannot get along with other people and find compatibility on some front especially with those we love, none of this will matter much.

What Erikson saw and came to believe is that the people in our immediate sphere, their attitudes toward the world and others, their own self-esteem, their perception of us, profoundly affect us. "Psychosocial," as explained earlier, is a word in two parts. The first part relates to the mind (psycho) and the second part relates to people with whom we interact (social). Erikson is purporting that our relationships help define who we are as individuals. The people we are most intimate with affect the way we think, what we believe about the world, and ultimately, about ourselves. In other words, the way we think affects how we interact. So our relationships, coupled with our DNA, amalgamate to create the life we live.

Stage 7—Middle Adulthood: Generativity vs. Stagnation

The Things We've Handed Down

My parents came from a generation that saw bragging on their kids as prideful and boasting. It was considered ill-mannered at least and downright rude at worst. The expectation was high regarding behavior and doing well in school. Reprimands were a felt duty; pride for the kids was rarely, if ever, verbalized because the focus was on correction. I, of course, tended along that unquestioned bent in my own parenting style without realizing it.

I especially recall the last dress rehearsal before a huge play the girls were in which involved lots of singing and dancing. They had practiced their hearts out and knew their parts to the letter. As we were leaving the auditorium to head home to get ready for the evening debut, a teacher stopped me. She wanted to apologize because my daughter's name had inadvertently been left off of the program. "Oh, that's okay," I demurred, "she gets more than her fair share of attention." My daughter was standing right there with me, taking it all in and, as I had done as a child, never questioning my reasoning.

I could have accepted the apology on her behalf or said something about how proud we were of her whether her name was in the program or not. I could have politely asked that they make a verbal correction after the performance. But, instead, I acted like it didn't matter. I remember this moment so vividly because even as I was saying this it didn't feel good. It pricked my conscience and caused me to begin to seriously question my propensity to react in this way.

Upon closer examination I was able to see that my mom's attitude about this had been handed down to me as if by osmosis. It permeated my mind and my being. Due to severe trauma in her own childhood, this cultural tendency was taken to extremes by my mom. Although this did change as she got older, when my mom was in her child-rearing years she would rarely, if ever, have thought to stand up for herself so she could not stand up for us. I got this even though it had never been told to me in words.

Fortunately, I chose to look at my propensities and began to change them, a process Erikson calls *Generativity. Stagnation*, on the other hand, occurs when people say (and I hear it often) "that's just the way I am. Get used to it." I see this attitude coming from fear. The fear comes from not knowing that you *can* change, from not knowing *how* to change. Being willing to look at that fear and ask for help is the task in this stage of life that moves us forward into happiness and fulfillment.

"Parenting doesn't come with an instruction manual," people often say. However, Erikson seems to have inadvertently given us at least a sort of structure from which to operate. Knowing what we're shooting for in each of these stages is what I have found to be immensely helpful. Just like the parents and students I've been involved with, I did so wish that I'd known this sooner.

Erikson's Stages of Psychosocial Development opened my eyes like nothing has before or since. No wonder I didn't know everything. I'm still going through life myself (and with a pretty huge deficit in some of the earlier stages). These stages provided a framework, some guidelines to what life was all about. I had a real and concrete reference point to which I could refer in order to help my kids move forward in their personal development.

The other part to this discovery, which was equally helpful, was that I, too, had decisions to make. I began to look at my own life in these stages of development and realized I had been through them with varying degrees of outcome. I was able to ask myself questions and I was not afraid to answer them honestly. An examination of my own adolescence began to foster self-forgiveness and self-empowerment. I began to look at my relationship to food as comfort, for example. Along this journey I was astonished to realize that my almost insatiable love for potato salad stemmed back to my childhood.

As a child, I had not much choice in matters surrounding my life. As an adult, I have all choice. I saw that I had made choices based on beliefs I held about myself. Some of these had been true, most had not.

For my purposes, one of the most important aspects of Erikson's research is that it allows adults to gain an understanding of themselves as well as their child. Since the stages cover the entire life span, this puts us all on the same playing field. We're all deciding what kind of life we will make for ourselves based on how we innately feel about our progress so far.

Stage 7 – Middle Adulthood		
"Am I satisfied with my life, or not?"	Middle Adulthood (40-60)	Generativity vs. Stagnation (Caring) The midlife crisis. Measure accomplishments/failures. Am I satisfied or not? Family and community are important and telling

Those who are able to move healthily through Stage 7 are those who are not afraid of change because they know that they have what it takes to make it. This is what Erikson calls *Generativity*. On the other hand, those who remain stuck in a relationship or job that isn't the best for them are in *Stagnation*. This is the term Erikson uses for someone who is willing to remain in an unsatisfactory state due to fear of failure.

For example, if you are in the *Middle Adulthood* stage and hate your current job as a shoe salesman in a large department store, you have some choices. You can stick with the job for the benefits and/or the money, not enjoying your profession and looking forward to your future only in light of retirement. Or, you can begin to look, dream and strategize, using your knowledge to open your own store or work in some other field completely. You can examine your state of dissatisfaction and realign your thinking.

Staying stuck means you are falling on the side of *Stagnation* on Erikson's scale. You blame others for your past ("if only I'd had the opportunity I'm giving my kids"). You also blame them for your present ("if I didn't have so much responsibility, I'd be able to do what I want").

Moving ahead with dreams and plans indicates an arrival on the healthy side of *Generativity* on Erikson's scale. You realize that your choices have been your own. You realize that you can move forward and still maintain a proper level of responsibility for your loved ones. One means you will be a victim, the other means you will be the victor in your own life story.

In my own case, my surprising inability to speak the truth on behalf of my kids, made me realize that I held some attitudes about myself as a parent that just didn't work. I came to see that some of these ideas stemmed from what my parents believed about the world, themselves and subsequently about their children. They instilled some permanent misconceptions in me and in my siblings based on their own particular culture and experience. For instance, both of my parents grew up during the Great Depression. This profoundly affected their experiences and for the most part, they lived as if it were still going on. There was always the worry of not having enough money and of not wasting food. This resulted in producing children with deep anxieties and various compulsions. It's not a blame game. They did the absolute best they could, just as I was doing. But, thanks to Erikson and other insights, my best got a whole lot better!

Stage 8—Late Adulthood: Integrity vs. Despair

Never Too Late

Helping our kids get along with other people while maintaining the integrity of their own identity is what this book is all about. The bottom line being: "The only thing that really matters in life are your relationships to other people." What a relief! This puts us all, parents and children alike, on the same playing field. Each is grappling with individual development or possibly the lack thereof.

When parents get this information, some admit that they have not taken the opportunity to fully develop their own personal identities. This makes parenting overly complex because of their own insecurities. For instance, if you are not comfortable with yourself or with your station in life, it becomes crucial to you that your kids perform well. It becomes important that they make you look good. Sometimes you may even depend on them to give your life meaning. When you are not secure in who you are as a person, it is so easy to take on parenting as an identity instead of a role.

Our identity is who we are at our core. Our role is our present function. Parenting is something you are doing right now. You will not always need to live with or parent your child. You will, however, always live with yourself.

Stage 8 – Late Adulthood		
"Am I proud of the life I've lived, or not?"	Late Adulthood (60-)	Integrity vs. Despair (Wisdom) This stage deals with looking back at legacy. Some handle the prospect of death well. Some can be bitter, unhappy. They reflect on the past and either conclude at satisfaction or despair.

Looking back on your life as you near its end will bring a feeling of either *Integrity* or *Despair* according to Erikson. These attitudes are based on how you feel you've lived your life in regard to your family, friends and your community at large. Have I left the world a better place? Are my most precious relationships intact? Are my children able to manage? Did I do a good job in taking care of myself? What can I do about it now?

We, and our children, must be able to navigate society in such a way that enhances our lives and the lives of those we love without harming others. At some point, our children grow up and they move on into their own autonomous lives. Allowing our children to discover who they are with our support and guidance is the biggest gift we can give to them—and to ourselves. And, the good news is that it's really never too late to begin doing that.

Bottom Line

Who you are right now as you read these words is a culmination of all of your life experiences. The way you approach life, how you feel about the situations and the people in your life at present began decades ago without your knowing it. Now you do.

Ask Yourself

Ask yourself how you've fared through each of these life stages. Write down your perceptions as you go back and look at each stage, at each crisis. As a child, who were your caregivers? How did you end up with them? Later in life, what were your self-perceptions at each stage that caused you to be with the people you chose to be with? Why did you, yourself, decide to become a parent? What were you hoping to gain? What have you enjoyed most about the experience? What have you enjoyed least?

Try This

Take a moment to write a letter to your nine-year-old self. Share your love and understanding for this little one. Reassure and encourage. Validate dreams. Forgive and bless.

Take a moment to write a letter to your 80-year-old self. Share your gratitude for the changes made in order to be happy and free. What are you most grateful for? What comfort do you take?

TAKE A BATH!

SECTION 2

Identity Crisis

"The privilege of a lifetime is being who you are."

Joseph Campbell

The Missing Link

One regular, normal day as I arrived home from work after collecting my son from wrestling practice, we each experienced our own giant leap of understanding through an ordinary but striking event. We got out of the car and headed toward the garage entrance of our house; I had only my purse but he was laden with a duffle bag full of equipment as well as his backpack bulging with the detritus of a busy school day. He was hot and sweaty and, being a wrestler, hungry as always. Wrestlers watch what they eat during the season so as not to be too heavy for their weight class.

As you probably know, teenage boys and hunger are not a good mix. He was frequently cranky, especially since my mom lived with us at the time and always had a mouth-watering pot of something simmering aromatically on her little stove downstairs.

Impatient to be done with the day, as he approached the garage door he began to attempt to kick off his shoes. All he wanted was to go inside, eat his plain baked potato, shower and sulk off to his room while the rest of us sat down to Hungarian goulash and toasted garlic bread straight from the oven.

Suddenly, he met with success as one of the stubborn shoes finally let go and went flying toward the garage door. We both stopped to watch the nice form and perfect arc of the airborne Nike's path. In an instant, the middle of the 3 glass panes of the garage door was shattered, falling to the driveway in a silver shower of tinkling glass. He froze. Slowly he turned to look at me in preparation for the usual barrage of condemnation. However, I had recently been introduced to the *Love & Logic®* philosophy and realized that I was being handed a golden opportunity on a big, fat silver platter.

This brilliant behavior management philosophy popular with leading educators and parents, first crossed my path during my last semester of graduate school in the form of a scratchy old VHS tape. This was the first and last piece of classroom management instruction I was to receive throughout the program. Up until then, all of the myriad classes on curriculum, pedagogy, developmental psychology, legal cases, and educational trends, had been conspicuously devoid of any training on how to manage a classroom.

Jim Fay, one of the original founders of the method, presented a cheery demeanor, can-do attitude, and, to my great relief, logical solutions to behavior problems both at school and at home. My joy, my rapture in finally seeing someone who had answers, who had an outlook that was fun as well as effective, was beyond measure. I can still feel that initial excitement even as I write these words. I felt like a castaway who'd been sighted by a Coast Guard vessel and I swam hard toward all of the *Love & Logic®* information I could get my hands on.

Here now, standing among shards of glass with my son, was a major moment, I realized, for both of us. So, instead of chastising and pointing out the extreme obvious with inane personal accusations like, oh, for instance, "What is the matter with *you?*" I simply stuck to the matter at hand: a broken window.

I looked at him with true surprise (at my collectiveness) and only a half smile (I didn't want him to see how happy I was about this situation) and I asked, "Wow, whatcha gonna do about that?"

He, of course, having been programmed in the art of self-defense-in-the-face-of-well-meaning-parents, reverted back to his training. "I didn't mean to, Mom." He was wide-eyed.

I continued my course, "Right, I can see that, but what will you do about it now?"

"But, I didn't mean to," he said, his faced screwed up in confusion and concern. "I know, sweetheart, I can see that you didn't mean to, but how are you going to fix it?" I saw what a good trainer I had been in helping him avoid responsibility. In his mind, he was clearly not responsible because it had been an accident. In the past, an accident like this would have resulted in his immediate punishment followed by my furious attempt to repair the damage.

"Mom!!!!" With an implanted stance, he dropped his bags, put both palms up and spoke as if I were hard-of-hearing. "I. Told. You. I. Did. Not. Mean. To. Do. It!"

Okay, now I felt truly sorry for him. I was definitely not playing by the long established rules. "Don't worry, honey, I'm not mad. I can help you find a glass company in the Yellow Pages and there are lots of things you can do around here to earn the money to pay for it."

His eyes began to fill with tears of frustration as he picked up his bags and we continued into the house. I remained calm but attentive, realizing that we were talking about glass here, not cancer. I saw his fear when he said, "I'm only 13 years old! I don't know *how* to talk to adults on the phone."

This was true. He had never had to speak to a perfect stranger in conducting business. He did not know that he had the complete capability to perform such an adult act because I had not yet expected him to be anything but a child. The machinations of the adult world were completely foreign to him. So, I set out to support him in this unplanned but crucial step from childhood into adulthood.

I gave him the name of the glass company that we had used in the past. He asked me what to say to them, then rang them up and said it. He put down the phone. "Fifty dollars?! I think I can do better than that." And, he proceeded to call other glass companies. As it turned out, he got a better price and the guys came that very day to do the repair. My son had enough cash saved to pay them in full right there on the spot. I never saw the repairmen. I stayed upstairs in the kitchen happily going about my evening chores but within reach if he should need assistance. I was proud. He was prouder. And, by the time his dad got home, my son had a much different story to tell about breaking the glass, one that would bring accolades and commendations rather than disappointment and reproach.

He had become one step closer to becoming a responsible adult because I had been provided with the tools that opened the avenue for passage. It was this melding of Erikson's research on the adolescent stage with the tools I was learning which provided the alchemy and basis for my work at home, in the classroom, and beyond.

Rites of Passage

Rites of passage are common in many cultures and used to be more so in our own. In the past, these simple and obvious rites clearly marked a child as having made the move to his or her adult role. In some cases, as with particular New Guinean tribes, when a boy climbed to the top of a tall, wooden tower and was able to conquer his fear and jump off with only a tether of goat leather strapped to his ankle, he was deemed an adult. The tether was strapped to the ankle of a child but loosed from the ankle of a man. This transition was clear to all in the village and celebrated accordingly. The transition from girl to woman was even simpler, facilitated by the onset of menses.

There was no trying to figure it out or trying to guess what constituted adulthood. The cultural expectation was that the child would pass on to become an adult which meant a contribution to family and society as well as a responsibility for the self.

Because our culture offers so few rites of passage into adulthood, there is no such clarity and no such expectation of responsibility in our present day society. Therefore, kids sometimes create their own. These are usually culturally unacceptable rites such as not coming home on time or at all, or cursing, or drinking, or smoking simply because they want to be adults and they perceive these as adult activities. Kids begin to copy adult behavior at a fairly young age. When I was six for instance, I was "smoking" my crayons and flicking the make-believe ashes out of the car window while my mom did the same with her real cigarettes. As with our attitudes about life, our habits are what our children pick up.

Think about it, the first real social responsibility that we allow a teenager in our culture today is to drive. Yep. We don't give them much to do before their 16th birthday but then we set them loose on society in a two-ton, mobile machine. In this light, is it really surprising that many teens see cars as over-sized toys? Is it any wonder then that the highest demographic for auto fatalities is teenagers?

Getting a driver's license is an example of a culturally accepted rite of passage that moves the teenager more into the adult role. This is as important for most teens as potty training is for toddlers. But there are many rites that could happen both within and without the household. Wouldn't it make sense to give your child more and more responsibility as they age so they are better prepared? Doesn't it make sense to recognize milestones in your child's life early on and to help them celebrate these accordingly? Wouldn't it be helpful for all involved to allow them to recognize and celebrate their accomplishments? In essence, it just makes sense to help one walk before expecting her to run.

Inabilities

Going Fishing

Anthony was a junior, a pleasant, easy-going kid with tousled blond hair and innocent blue eyes who never had a bit of trouble in school. He was a likeable normal kid whose parents were going through a bitter divorce and there was so much acrimony in Anthony's life that he became despondent. At first, he became increasingly reluctant to get out of bed in the morning for school. Then, on the days that he did make it to school, he was not engaged in any of his classes. While not unpleasant or belligerent to students or teachers, he smiled as he went from class to class, but he seemed to be someplace else.

When his grades began to suffer, it did not bother him at all. Still pleasant and biddable, he never complained to his parents or mentioned any melancholy. He was a good kid. He knew his parents were miserable and had no intention of adding fuel to the fire. For all of their experience and education (his mother was a counselor, his father, a psychotherapist), his parents were so emotionally entangled in the divorce dispute that they couldn't see the forest for the trees. Like many of us, their actions produced a different result than their intentions.

In an effort to get him back on track, his mother petitioned for a transfer to the alternative school for the last 3 months of the school year. She was at her wits' end and had hoped a move would help him to focus on his studies. His father reluctantly agreed although he felt Anthony just needed to buckle down and get back to it and certainly did not need a "special" school. Anthony ended up in my class and continued much the same as he had before. Finally, with two weeks left in the school year, I had an honest talk with his dad who had called to talk to me about our apparent failure to curb Anthony's continued apathy.

"Dr. Davis," I said hesitantly into the phone. "Anthony is in no danger of failing the 11th grade. His grades are by no means stellar, but he will pull through. He seems very sad to me and he has mentioned that what he misses most is going fishing with you. Would you consider pulling him out of school and going on a fishing trip?"

"I hardly think that would help his grades and besides there are only two weeks of school left." He was confused and rankled by a teacher recommending this course of action.

"Exactly. Only two weeks and he's already passed." There was a long silence as something struck a chord and his voice became quietly hopeful. "Do you really think that would help?"

Anthony was unable to balance his emotions with the expectations his parents had for him around school. He had been a good student throughout all of his previous school life. His story is a really good example of how inabilities can affect us. Most inabilities are temporary and can stem from a range of causes like lack of sleep or depression. These are issues that can be readily addressed once they are identified.

Many of the parents I work with share the common complaint that their child is misbehaving. It's usually what brings them to me in the first place. This misbehavior comes in many forms. Sometimes the kids are acting up in class or not completing assignments. Sometimes they don't come home on time or they treat their parents disrespectfully. Sometimes they are compliant but not meeting parental expectation in one way or another as in the case of Anthony. Dealing with symptoms instead of the underlying problem is a common occurrence in parenting and it is as helpful as treating a serious bronchial infection with mere cough syrup. Anthony was sad about his parents' divorce and because he missed his father. Making good grades, doing well in school, was not the answer to making him feel better.

When parents would appear in my workshop because their children were truant, I made it clear from the outset that I would be helping them deal with the problem that caused this truancy. The judge, I pointed out, is interested in remedying truancy, which I considered to be the symptom of an underlying issue.

Delving into these issues brought up many things. A sixth grader was morbidly obese and yet his mother refused to address this issue and continued to call the police to help her get her child out of the house and to school. A ninth-grade girl was actually on an Individual Education Plan due to extreme anxiety and yet her grandparents, who were raising her, reluctantly allowed her to skip school instead of seeking treatment for her affliction.

Very often the root of obesity or anxiety is deep-seated and may stem from emotional wounds or childhood traumas. These things will not go away unless addressed, no matter how much we may want them to. I encourage parents to educate themselves regarding the primary issue at hand and to allow their children to be educated about themselves. This calls for bravery and extreme valor on the part of parents. It may require testing or other assessments. But often times just being aware of basic information like the effects of birth order or differing learning styles has great benefit. Sometimes there is a temporary issue like depression or other illness, or an undetected learning disability, which almost always leads to the serious issue of a distorted self-image if allowed to go undetected.

Disabilities

"I just can't get it like everyone else can."

For most of his elementary and middle school life my son came home with comments on his report card noting that he was "very social" (he had kind teachers). His grades generally lagged just a bit behind what we all felt they could be. He was busy at school with sports and friends but not with school work and he insisted time and time again that he was "dumb." "I just can't get it like everyone else can."

Early on, when I was that parent who nagged and scolded, I tended to try to convince him otherwise and I was never beneath threatening. Yet, I was assured at parent/teacher conferences that he was bright but needed to settle down to the task at hand.

Finally, when he was in middle school, I realized that whether he lacked the ability to do well in school or not, he believed this to be true. This was validated by his less than average grades and therefore furthered his belief in his inability. Neither I, nor his teachers, could convince him otherwise. So, I decided to have him tested, even though this had never been suggested by his teachers who firmly believed, as did his dad and I, that he just needed to "buckle down." I had exhausted all other avenues: scolding, nagging, comparing, "helping" with homework, punishing, tutors, reading programs, you name it and we had over the years tried it. The tests came back with no surprises to me but he was very surprised to find that his intelligence was above average and that he had no learning disability. He was right up against the borderline of Attention Deficit Disorder but he did not truly meet the criteria for that diagnosis.

Having this information was extremely powerful. We began to realize that changes in diet and study habits helped. We communicated these findings to his teachers and so he lost his excuse of helplessness both at home and at school.

But the most important change was in his ability to see himself differently. And, yes, this was a practice. Over time, he would see that doing his schoolwork or not was a choice. It was his choice. When he had believed himself to be "dumb," he honestly felt he had no choice, and that he was consistently being asked to perform at a level that he could not achieve.

The truth is that he really missed this excuse and he was so used to using it that he became a bit resentful. I remember when he came home with a 'D' on his report card. Instead of nagging, I asked how he felt about this knowing that he was smart enough to make a better grade. He shrugged, "I don't care."

"Will you care when all of your friends are in eighth grade and you are left in the seventh grade next year? With the sixth graders?" He had told me time and time again how these little sixth graders were just clueless.

Then I saw it. I saw that little light pass over his eyes, that glimmer of the recognition of truth. Yet, he shrugged again dismissively. I understood this. I got that he couldn't really say that I, the grown up, was right. I was satisfied in the knowledge that change would come. He would become the student he could be and I would become the parent I wanted to be. It was a win–win.

My son's problem was not mediocre grades. His problem was his self-image. He believed that he was not smart and his grades reflected this belief back to him. The grades were a symptom. His long held self-image as a mischievous, not-too-smart clown was the problem. Inappropriate behavior was a symptom. His conviction that he could do no better was the problem.

As you may imagine, parents who generally end up calling on me are those who have tried everything they know to make the situation better. Calling for help is a humbling and often desperate measure and one that I commend highly. It's a brave, bold stroke on their part.

Because I am not a clinician, I often suggest to those parents, who feel they are at their wits' end, that they have their child assessed. Sometimes the child is having difficulty maintaining grades; sometimes they are having difficulty maintaining friends and other social connections. You can probably guess some of the responses I get to this recommendation. Here are the 3 most common:

"I don't want my kid labeled!"

"I don't want to put my kid on meds!"

"I don't want him to be able to use a diagnosis as an excuse not to perform!"

So, I ask, "If your child had been born blind, would you send him off to school day after day and tell him to suck it up, to try harder, to learn how to fit in? Would you say, 'I'm sick to death of cleaning up your scrapes and bruises; stop running into walls for Pete's sake?"

Right. You can see where I'm going here. If you knew there was an issue, you'd address it with a walking cane, with specialized training, or with books he could actually read.

Even if you feel there's nothing wrong, I tell parents, you can do it for your own peace of mind. You may discover, like I did, that there are other issues to be addressed with no need of a diagnosis. Educating yourself and your child can never hurt if the information is used rightly.

Learning Styles

Paper Airplanes in Math Class

When I was in third grade and meant to be learning multiplication tables, I had a teacher named Mrs. Harris. Mrs. Harris was long in the tooth by the time I got to her as her crooked mouse-grey wig and bleeding Avon lipstick could attest. Now, it's obvious to me that she was passively awaiting retirement and really should have been put out to pasture long before. But back then, I was taught to believe that teachers were smart and right. Always.

As Mrs. Harris had no blood, she was perpetually chilly even when it was 95 degrees outside. After lunch, when she did switch on the one box fan assigned to our unairconditioned classroom, the drone of white noise was like the song of the Sirens luring the class to la-la land. While our tummies were full and our senses were otherwise engaged in digestion, we listened to 45 rpm records. "1x1 is 1," and the class would sing out in rote response,"1x1 is 1." My classmates' eyes glazed over like bored parishioners intoning the liturgy in the glare of the Louisiana sun while our noses dripped perspiration onto our desktops.

It was *so* painful! Even though Mrs. Harris chose this time to prop herself up in the corner and nap, I knew I couldn't leave my desk to shake my classmates awake because that was against the rules. So, I did my best to help with my newly found skill of making and flying paper airplanes. After all, I wasn't paying the least bit of attention so why not be helpful and try to tap Scott or Sheila in the head. I must admit I was a pretty good aim.

So, it wasn't only Mrs. Harris who was stunned when her left eyelid lifted slowly to survey the room only to see a flash of white sail across the aisles. I, too, was completely shocked when she loudly and tersely called my name. At least now everybody was awake.

She held her bony finger up and curled it repeatedly toward her nose, gesturing for me to come to her. I slowly peeled the backs of my damp little legs from my desk seat, fingering the hem of my dress while I kept a smile glued on my face, a very well learned personal defense tactic against crying that she mistook for insolence. Upon my approach, she pursed her lips which made her rigid chin jut out like Frankenstein's other aunt. Her blood-red lipstick followed deep, long ruts halfway to her nose. She turned her veined hand over and jerked her index finger downward toward the floor in front of her. I plopped cross-legged onto the cool tile.

This situation was to become routine. I just could not bear the boredom and I knew I wasn't supposed to be sleeping! I spent most of third grade math class staring at Mrs. Harris' white-cottoned crotch beneath the thick polyester skirt that bridged her knobby knees. I tried staring at her glinting diamond ring. I watched as she covertly massaged her aching joints. I studied her rolled down stockings and her thick-soled lace-ups. I even traced a few varicose veins, all to no avail. I could not help trying to peek over my shoulder to see how my classmates were coming along which would get me a nudge from her shoe even though her eyes were shut.

Testing is one of the things that could have helped but I wasn't behind academically and I was socially on target. I was meeting and surpassing all other benchmarks measured through standardized testing and I was not ordinarily a troublemaker. So, I grew up from that time forth with a debilitating mental block around math. I didn't know my multiplication tables and so math, from then on, was excruciating.

I can look back on my own life and school experience and see that I became the class clown out of sheer boredom. Most teaching styles did not engage my interest. I believe I would have in most cases found the information intriguing as I do have a curious mind and love learning. But now I can look back and see that had my teachers and my parents, understood the style in which I learned best, I would have learned more. As it was, a very bright little girl, came away truly perceiving herself as not being able to know as much as everyone else.

Years of dimmed self-esteem and pain could possibly be avoided by educating yourself and your child regarding learning style. Does she learn by hearing (auditory), by seeing (visual), by doing (kinesthetic), or all of the above? There are oodles of information on learning styles available on every level, and helping children to understand this could keep them from running aground in school where a large part of their self-image is initially shaped.

The good news is that, especially in the adolescent stage, we can begin to address our preconceived notions and begin to look inside ourselves for our true identity. Helping someone discover innate talents and gifts and sensibilities is a gift in and of itself. For me, this has been the absolute most rewarding aspect of parenting and teaching.

Birth Order

Sister, Sister

Recently, I was recounting an incident that happened when I was a child. My oldest sister, upon hearing this, observed that my memory of our childhood certainly didn't jibe with hers. I agreed. She's the oldest and I'm the youngest. Although we lived in the same household and were raised by the same parents, we had very different experiences. She, as the oldest girl was given much more responsibility than I, as the youngest, had ever gotten. The expectation was that she would see to chores in a way that was not expected of me.

When we were younger, my siblings thought that I was treated better than they were by our parents. They saw this as unfair even though they constantly watched out for me and cared for my needs because I was "the baby." Now that my sister has grown children of her own, she has a bit of a different perspective.

Her older children accuse her of having treated her youngest in a way that was unfair to them. "You never spent that kind of money on us," is one of the more common themes. My sister tries to explain that she and their dad had practically no money when they began having kids and their situation greatly improved over the years. "If I could've, I would've," she tells them although it doesn't seem to assuage their long held feelings that may have more to do with perception than reality.

Parenting, just like any other role you have in life, can be done more effectively if you know and understand who or what you're dealing with. Dr. Kevin Lehman helped me, long before I had kids, to better understand my propensities based on where I fell in my own family of siblings. Later, this knowledge helped me to understand my own children. It was very useful in relating to my students as well.

Decades ago, Dr. Lehman wrote *The Birth Order Book* which explains many of our tendencies and dispositions in light of whether we are the only, oldest, middle or youngest child. I was convinced he was onto something when I began perusing the book from the back and read, "if you're the youngest, you're probably starting this book here." I stopped reading and looked over my shoulder. Seriously? How did he know that?

When I began using this information in my classroom, I did some casual research of my own. I discovered that most of the kids who ended up in my class of expelled students were middle children. These are the kids who generally do things differently and often they end up going against the grain, even to their own detriment.

There are many variables such as gender and time spans between births but basically here is what it boils down to:

Only or Oldest: High achievers. Most U.S. Presidents have been oldest or only children.

Middle: Think outside the box. Bill Gates is a middle child.

Youngest: Comfortable with attention and performing. Many comedians, including Billy Crystal, are youngest.

You can gain quick insight into your own style of being as well as your child's. This can help you begin to honor and respect your child in light of the forces that helped shape her into who she has become. More importantly, you will be able to use this information for her and not against her; thereby, becoming the parent you have always wanted to be.

Like Erikson before him, Dr. Lehman has simply observed a cultural phenomenon. The effects of birth order are generalizations and there are those who don't readily fit the norm.

For example, most of my kids fit the expected generalities. But, Tim, while being the oldest of my children, exhibits the tendencies of an only child. This could be accounted for by the 6-year gap between him and the second born. Or, it could be because they never lived together as a family during his developmental years.

The fourth born child exhibits many characteristics of a youngest child. I attribute this to gender. She may have been the fourth born but she is the youngest girl. Two boys came after her so she has some of the care-taking propensities of an older child as well.

It is believed that our order of birth affects all of our relationships. You can see how an oldest child and a youngest child make a good match as partners. In simplest terms, the oldest is comfortable caring for others and the youngest is comfortable being cared for.

Birth order is a fun thing to look at in your children. It can be a useful tool in understanding how children brought up under the same roof, by the same parents, with many of the same experiences, can end up being so vastly different from each other.

Birth order, learning styles, the presence of a learning disability, or a temporary inability such as depression, all affect the way we think about ourselves. These add to the complexity of who we are as people and many times drive our behaviors and attitudes. The more awareness we have around these facets of our being, the more capable we are of changing situations that don't work for us.

Remember what Jesus said? "As a man thinks in his heart, so shall he be." Now science is bearing out what mystics and religious scholars have contended for millennia. We really do become who we feel we are. Feelings are that part of us which by many accounts override our intellect. Think of the times when you've made some unexplainable decision and then smacked yourself on the head V-8 style, "What was I thinking?" My guess is that your were reacting to your true feelings which sometimes are *very* buried within what we suppose we should, ought, or need to be. Self-knowledge brings with it a certain enlightenment that ultimately leads to freedom.

Conduct Your Own Right of Passage

The fifth stage on Erikson's graph is the one that holds so much power. It's the point where we have the opportunity as well as the ability to become our own person and to begin to take responsibility for our own decisions. It is the place where we can become victors instead of victims if the adults in our lives (our significant others) are willing and able to allow us to live with our choices. As with so many parents with whom I've worked, I realized that I had deficiencies in my own identity development that impeded my ability to logically respond to the needs of my children.

ERIKSON'S 8 PSYCHOSOCIAL STAGES OF DEVELOPMENT – STAGE 5 - ADOLESCENCE		
"Do I know who I am, or not?"	Adolescence (Puberty)	Identity vs. Identity Confusion (Fidelity) Questioning of self. Who am I? How do I fit in? Where am I going in life? Erikson believes that children allowed to explore and conclude their own identity will not face identity confusion. Those who are continually pushed to conform to another's views will face identity confusion.

So, I went back to the adolescent stage and pulled myself up by my bootstraps so that I could get on with the business of life with my most precious relationships intact. I took a look at how my self-perception shaded every relationship I had with other people, places and things. I was able to see clearly and quickly that I had aged out of the adolescent stage with no firm identity. I, like many of us, could not look back and point to one moment in time when I went from being a girl to being a woman. I went back to re-examine my life in terms of when I had begun to take responsibility for my own decisions. Was it when I left home, when I got married, when I got my first job, or when I became a parent myself? I began to see that although I had done all of these things, I still gave my power to others by blaming them for any lack of contentedness that I felt. If everyone would just behave, I'd be fine!

The realization that I alone was responsible for my own happiness, led to my enrolling myself in therapy, facing some truths about my career and marriage, joining other groups in terms of looking at propensities and making changes that were at times uncomfortable to both me and my family. The shoe through the glass scene with my son is a case in point. It eventually dawned on me that it was not my job to adjust my kids to my own level of satisfaction, nor was it *my* place to deal with *their* issues. This is their right and their privilege as they occupy their own space in the world.

I began to help my kids move toward forming their own identities, by supporting and understanding the necessity of their forward motion, instead of pulling them back ("for their own good") as they tried to expand into themselves. I began to get myself up to speed in my own development and began to forgive myself for not being what I could not have been in the past. I began to come into my own personal power, with the realization that I, and I alone, have power over my life, my decisions, my choices, my outcomes and most importantly, my attitudes. I could no longer blame a deficit in the quality of my life on kids coming home late, or a stalled career or lack of opportunity. My life was my responsibility and mine alone.

Eventually, I became a trained *Love & Logic®* facilitator and began to conduct workshops for parents. In so doing, I made a crucial discovery: those parents who seem to have healthily made it through their own developmental stages, whose identities as people are intact, are better able to grasp the tools they need to help their kids. On the other hand, by the time their kids are teens, many parents are so embroiled emotionally in power struggles with their kids and others that their resentment and anger interfere with the logic aspect of the program. They see themselves as victims of their kids' behaviors because they see themselves as victims in their own lives.

Erikson's stages become the basic jumping off point for understanding. This new information sometimes prompts parents to sit back in their chairs with a look of wonder and/or horror, "I have not completed my own adolescent stage. No wonder I can't help my kid!"

The opportunities for passage from childhood to adulthood, from dependency to responsibility, come daily. They come in the form of broken windows or larger occurrences such as handing over the keys to your car for the first time. The basic idea is to allow your child to realize potential, to step into their capabilities whether it's making their own school lunch or driving your other kids to school.

There are other ways to walk into *your* true self as well. Often, we grow up with innate propensities that cause us to act or react in certain ways. Many components affect our outlook: birth order, learning styles, learning disabilities, illness, the way in which we've been taught to deal with disappointments or hurts.

The good news is that this realization can lead you to come to grips with your own developmental shortfall. Some of you may enter therapy or marriage counseling; some may begin to deal with your own addictions to food, control, attention, success, drugs or to adrenaline, or you may have yourselves assessed for an as yet undiagnosed learning disability. You will begin to lead from a better understanding of yourself and your children. In a sense, you will conduct your own rite of passage into responsible adulthood. Discovering and allowing yourself to be who you really are, will allow you to let your kids do the same.

Bottom Line

You were born with a DNA package that contains all kinds of propensities, gifts, abilities and ways of processing information. Events in your life such as accidents, illness, trauma, your role in the family, affect the brain and your heart responses. Knowing these things about yourself can help you move forward into your own truth. This enriches your life and ultimately the life of your child.

Ask Yourself

How well do I really know myself? Have I taken an honest look at my talents, my abilities, my fears, my insecurities, my self doubts? In what ways have I compensated for some of my propensities? How have my attributes affected the way in which I parent?

Try This

Take a moment to write about the role you played in your family of origin. What were the expectations? Did the expectations of your family fit with who you were?

Take a moment to write about the role you play currently in your family? What are the expectations? Are you comfortable with what's expected of you?

Now answer these questions in regard to your child.

TAKE A BATH!

SECTION 3

How To Break the Anger Cycle

"The power is in you. The answer is
in you. It's never outside."

Eckhart Tolle

The Naïve Anger Cycle

What Ever Happened to Baby John?

My son, John, is the youngest of our children. At this writing he is 25 years old, lives on the other side of the world, has his Master's Degree, stands nearly 6 feet tall, and yet we still call him "Baby John." I'm not sure if this is a Southern thing or just a youngest thing but it seems quite common for most members of a family to see the youngest as the perpetual family pet. The youngest is loved and doted on in trickle-down fashion, which usually contributes to the fostering of a biddable, enjoyable personality. "Baby John" is no exception.

He got lots of kisses and lots of attention growing up and his siblings still feel a bit protective of him. Also, it didn't hurt that he was so cute as a toddler; perfect strangers often stopped us to coo at him. As with most cabooses, he was good-natured and funny and was good at laughing his way out of sticky situations. So, imagine my surprise when, one day, he did not respond in the charming, if not acquiescent, manner to which I had grown accustomed.

At this point John was 11. I should have been waiting for this stage with open mind and open arms but you must remember that I was somewhere toward the bottom of my learning curve at this point in my parenting.

I simply asked John, on this particular day, why he hadn't taken out the trash. I got a petulant mumble in response. So, as I was wont to do back then, I began to verbally tick off all of the reasons why he should take out the trash in a timely manner, chief of which was that I was sick and tired of telling him to do so. This was not an unfamiliar little tirade; I'm sure John could have quoted me verbatim. So instead of obediently standing there and listening to me yet once again, he spun on his heels and proceeded to walk out of the kitchen.

"John!" I barked as he headed toward the stairs to go down to his room.

He continued to walk away from me. Not only that, he was *mocking* me: "blah, blah, blah, blah . . ." he said with his arms waving in the air.

"John!!" I followed him, rounding the corner just as he was making his way down the stairs continuing his blah, blah, blahing.

In my helplessness to stop him, my temper flared. Seriously flared. If my head had been a thermometer the mercury would have literally shot out the top of my skull, and the only way I could think to stop him was to push him down the stairs. This was not really a thought so much as an impulse. Fortunately, I knew that wasn't the right thing to do but the fact that it had flashed through my mind was mortifying.

Up to this point in life, I had been a master at internalizing my anger so this rage that I felt outwardly was as unexpected as it was unwanted. I'd gotten openly perturbed and irritated before, lots of times. But, I'd never raged or screamed or thrown things or hit people, much less pushed them down to get their attention.

What bothered me most about this incident was my lack of understanding. How could I feel such extreme irritation toward anyone, much less toward someone I loved and adored? And over taking out the trash?! This was mystifying to say the least, but in retrospect, not totally surprising. All I had learned about anger, up to this point, was that it was a bit like stepping in a hole. So, losing my temper was something I was careful not to do because I had not been taught how to get out of that hole once I got in it. Therefore, getting angry was to be avoided at all costs. Being that out of control emotionally with nowhere to go, with no way to back your self out, is terrifying. I certainly did not want to hurt people and I did not want to do or say things that I knew I'd regret. But, mainly, I never wanted to be that out of control.

I had grown up seeing my daddy burst into flames and roar like a Christmas bonfire when someone tailed his pickup too closely, or went the speed limit in front of him, or otherwise "made" him mad. Through the actions of my family, I was taught to understand that anger couldn't be helped, that the subsequent language and behaviors were just flung upon us, much like a sudden craving. As a child, it was awful to witness this especially in a parent. I was left to guess that anger just had to work its course. I learned to become invisible until the coast was clear again.

Imagine my surprise, then, when I got to my first real teaching job in the program run by Joyce and Gloria, and was expected to teach the *Social Survival Skills* curriculum, the main premise of which is that anger is actually a choice. (Say what?) It is a secondary response based on primary emotions. (Huh?) I know, hard to believe, right?

Our internal gauges run a vast gamut of human emotion. I imagine my own gauge as a ratcheted line running from my pelvis to my skull. Most of us have little to no knowledge of how to identify and name the myriad feelings that run up and down this thing all day long like a manic elevator, so we stop on those most familiar to us, usually happy, angry or sad. These we readily recognize.

I learned that anger most often stems from some *other* emotion like hurt or fear or embarrassment. These are some of the lesser respected feelings, and are often times seen as weak so we aren't as attuned to them. In fact many of us are taught to ignore these and other feelings except in their extremes. Anger, on the other hand, is easily recognizable and often glorified in our culture. For most of us, it seems much less scary to get mad and stomp off rather than admit hurt and cry. However, if we can identify the basic feeling of our discomfort, we can deal with *that* one and not have to go to anger, unless we find it necessary and fitting for the situation at hand.

When we aren't in touch with our true feelings, the little elevator zooms right by them until we get to the more familiar ones where it comes to a jolting halt. This happens in a millisecond, which is why it can be so hard for some parents to believe at first.

"No, Terri," they say, "I get pissed off instantly when something happens. There is *nothing* that comes first."

This behavior is called the Naïve Anger Cycle. We are unaware that there are primary feelings and so there's no way we can identify them. Clueless as to how to react in any other way, we go straight to anger. The following diagram is fairly simple and easy to understand. I'll use the experience of a former student of mine in explanation of the terms.

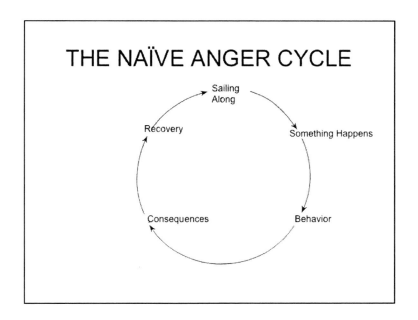

I Ain't Goin' to Your Party Dude

Oliver was a big kid. Always tall for his age, with a soft and pleasant manner, he had been repeatedly teased throughout his school career. By the time he reached high school, he towered over his peers and was a regular target for those boys needing to prove their machismo. This resulted in many fights and the continual hardening of Oliver's demeanor.

One day, at the beginning of his senior year, Oliver was in the hallway at school (Sailing Along) when, out of the blue, a kid began berating him and ultimately took a swing at him (Something Happens). Oliver was enraged and hit the kid back, *hard* (Behavior). The kid's jaw was hurt and Oliver was expelled from school (Consequence). He ended up in my class for the first half of his senior year (Recovery).

121

The Aware Anger Cycle

I n my class, Oliver, along with his classmates, was introduced to another possible course of action in the form of what we call the Aware Anger Cycle.

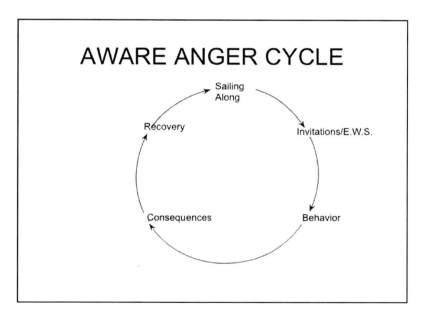

As you can see, in this version, "Something Happens" becomes "Invitations." Throughout the semester, Oliver gained the understanding that anything that happens to him is an invitation only and, like any invitation, can be accepted or rejected. This realization allows for a major shift in perspective. Suddenly, Oliver had power over his actions instead of allowing himself to fall victim to someone else's choices.

Some invitations are verbal and some are physical. Some are positive and some are negative. The class came up with several examples of each such as, "I love you," and "Shut up," in the verbal category. Gestures, such as a friendly wave as well as flipping someone off, made the physical category.

You'll notice, too that "Early Warning Signs (E.W.S.)" has been added to this cycle. Here is where we begin to pay attention to our physical reactions which clue us in to what is going on inside of us.

Eventually, Oliver was able to realize that in these situations his cheeks got hot and his palms became sweaty before he got mad. These were physical signs he had never paid attention to. He was able to begin to then pay attention to and recognize early emotions such as fear and hurt and nervousness in any potentially volatile situation.

Oliver returned to his school after winter break in hopes of graduating on time. This meant that he had to pass every class. He was very conscious of the fact that he had a lot at stake and had decided that getting into trouble would not be an option for him. His future took precedence.

On his first day back while he stood at his locker chatting with his buddies (Sailing Along), a friend of the sore-jaw boy purposely knocked into Oliver (Invitation). This time, Oliver rubbed his palms together noticing the dampness (Early Warning Sign) and remembered what hung in the balance. He looked down his nose at the boy, who was already in a fighting stance, smiled and responded to the "Invitation" with a line that he, himself, had come up with in our class. He calmly said,

"I ain't goin' to your party, dude," and turned away (Behavior). Oliver felt completely powerful (Consequence) as he walked down the hall toward his next class, leaving the stunned kid staring after him. I know this because his mother called to tell us what happened and to thank us. Obviously, this course of action required no "Recovery" time.

This method of understanding anger leaves no room for self-victimization. Yes, you may accept invitations and choose to ignore early warning signs, but the choice becomes yours. No matter what you choose, you get to live with the positive *or* negative consequences that are dependent on *your* actions.

Anger is often a major issue in parenting. Either we're blowing up at the kids or they're blowing up at us, or both. Many of us truly believe that if we're angry, it's because of someone else's nonsensical behavior. If the other person would just straighten up, then all would be well and we could go on about our right and proper business. Yet what I've come to see is that when I'm angry, it's *my* problem and not anyone else's. As with anything in life, when we blame another person, we give up all of our own power and are no longer in control of our own lives or experiences.

Think of all the times you've said or heard something like, "he made me so mad . . ." Think about that statement. When someone can "make" you do anything then obviously you are not in control of your own life. You are here, holding your personal space on the earth, with all of the ability to create your own experiences. Why, then, would you promptly give up that right and hand your behavior over to someone else like a puppet on a string?

With as many mistakes as I've made over the years, I'm always happy to think of a time where I may have helped my kids move further along in life rather than causing them a hindrance. One such bright event happened in the midst of a very dark one and had to do with my daughter, who at the time was also a senior in high school. By this time, I had been teaching and using this information daily so I was ready.

I was at the stove making dinner after a long day of work (SAILING ALONG). I got a call from a nice security guard at the local department store saying my 17-year old daughter was being retained there after being caught with stolen merchandise (INVITATION). My heart began to race, my voice quavered, my stomach churned and my hands shook as I hung up the phone (EARLY WARNING SIGNS). I called her dad and left to meet him at the store to retrieve her. When I saw her sitting in the dim little security office with tears in her eyes, I was hopeful. She rarely if ever shared feelings with us unless it was anger or annoyance and I intuitively knew that this was a good sign. After our brief meeting with store security, she rode back with me. On the drive home I said to her, "I'm not saying anything because I honestly don't know what to say" (BEHAVIOR). All the things I could think of I knew were useless and after seeing her tears, I had vowed to take special care with my words.

Once we got home, she went to her room while my husband and I conferred in our bedroom. He was really upset. I shared with him my belief that this could be an opportunity for her and that the usual parental screeching and lamenting would do her no good. I had done my share of this in the past with her due to my own fears and not knowing what else to do. While we were talking, she suddenly appeared in the doorway. We asked her to come in and sit. Not sure what to say, I opened my mouth in trepidation. But before I could say anything, she burst into tears and sobs which shocked me. We had never seen this from her. I sat on the bed amazed at my ability to watch her in intense emotional pain while at the same time knowing that this was a breakthrough.

"What is it, sweetheart? What's wrong?" I sensed that this was not totally a response to the incident. It took a few minutes for her to get through the wrenching sobs. We waited.

"It's just that I've never felt like I've belonged. All the other kids are fine and fit in but I have never felt that way. Not even when I was little. Sometimes I don't even feel like I fit in with them. It just seems that I'm different."

This obviously went very deep into her heart and into her past. I was in over my head, something I'd felt with her many times before. Only this time, I realized my limitations. We thanked her for being so open with us and acknowledged that it had not been easy.

So instead of saying all the things I would have said at one time: How could you do this? What were you thinking? Do you realize how mortifying this is for us? Haven't we taught you better? Etc., etc., and so forth, I was able to be honest about my own feelings and to admit that I was at a loss.

"I'm afraid for you. And, I don't know how to help you. We've tried counseling but your weren't ready. But, the fact is that had you been 18 already, you would have been calling us from jail and would have a permanent criminal record." Her birthday was later in the year; she was listening.

"I know it was a stupid thing to do." She was so sad.

"It seems to me that your getting to the bottom of why you did it is important." This was not the first time she'd taken things and we had caught her being dishonest more than once. In those past times she'd been angry, hostile and non-communicative; this time it was different. She was open and vulnerable. "Honestly honey, trying to love you has been like trying to force feed an anorexic. I just don't know how to help you."

Her dad told her that we were not going to punish her because we felt this had been punishing enough. He further emphasized his hope that she would get help in gaining insight into her own behaviors. This was the first truly heartfelt dialogue we ever had (CONSEQUENCE).

The conversation was enlightening both to her and to us as we discussed her perception of our parenting and her siblings. We were able to put ourselves in a position to support her efforts to explore her own behaviors and the emotions behind them (RECOVERY).

I tell you this story with my now grown daughter's permission and with all humility. Had it happened even six months prior, I would have had a very different response because I could not have made a *choice* to be angry or not. In this situation, I was able to look at my underlying emotions. I was able to allow myself to feel fear (Where would such behavior lead?), sadness (Why does she feel she can't ask for what she wants?), embarrassment (I have failed as a parent and now everyone will know), and remorse (If only I had known these things and been more understanding).

Now, the truth is that I could have felt all of these emotions and chosen to allow myself to become indignant and to get angry anyway. But because of all I'd learned, I knew that she didn't have the tools to do any better. She had been raised by her grandmother and had never lived with her siblings in Vietnam. She had not ever been close to her biological mother. She was collected at the last minute and under shrieks and screams of protest made the trek across the ocean with a group of near strangers (her family). She had had a growing infection throughout most of her childhood that resulted in immediate surgery once she got to the states. Therefore, her tolerance for both emotional and physical pain is unbelievable and she had no reason to expect that others would care for her needs. She had become a survivor at age four.

This is such a deep memory for me because this daughter whom I love so much had long suffered in silence. Early on, she had caused me to seek counseling in an effort to help her when she appeared to not want help or input from anyone. Now, she was in talking to us and sharing such painful and deeply held emotions. I know, in my heart of hearts, that had I taken the old clueless route to child-rearing, we would have ended with harsh words, slammed doors and recriminations which would have led to further humiliation, resentment, quite possibly harmful behavior on her part and further helplessness on mine. Recovery would have been about the survival of our relationship, our ability to coexist, and not about her own personal development and progress.

This story exemplifies one of the things I've learned to appreciate about parenting. We get lots of chances to practice. Our kids help us in this way. And the real beauty of this is that we learn by helping them learn. It's a win-win, baby!

Bottom Line

Anger is a subject of extensive study and research, written about and discussed ad nauseum. It has its time and its place. It had no place in the story that I just shared; yet, you can see how it could've easily taken precedence. Anger is in essence a fight or flight response and is best used to remove us from dangerous or unhealthy situations. When we learn to use anger rightly, we can navigate our own lives. We can see clearly to steer our lives into safe and clean emotional waters.

I have come to see anger simply as jet fuel, both powerful and useful and possibly dangerous. It is a form of energy that is to be burned up as it propels us away from unhealthy situations. It is not meant to be used in the punishment or chastisement of ourselves or of another. Nor is it meant to be stored inside of us where it can continue to burn to our emotional and physical detriment.

Ask Yourself

Take a look at a past circumstance where your angry reaction has caused you a painful and long recovery period. With that thought in mind and using the Naïve Anger Cycle, identify where you were. School? Work? Traffic? Home? This is the place where you were "Sailing Along," minding your own business. "Something Happened" which caused you to get angry. What was that? Fill in the blank there as well. Next, identify your "Behavior" and "Consequences" in the appropriate spots. What was the resulting "Recovery Time?" It could be that you are still in this recovery time.

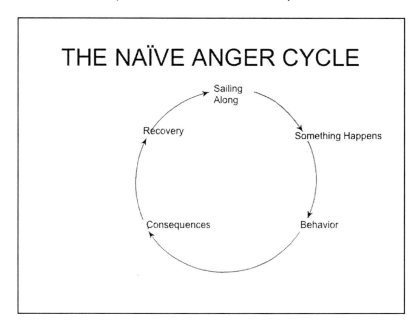

THE NAÏVE ANGER CYCLE

Sailing Along

Something Happens

Behavior

Consequences

Recovery

Try This

Now, let's take a look at the same situation with your current awareness. Using the Aware Cycle, fill in the blanks beginning with the same instance. This time, though, think about what you felt before you got angry. What did you feel emotionally? Were you embarrassed, nervous, anxious, afraid? Be sure to identify not just the feeling, but the object of your feeling as well. For instance, instead of just writing "I was afraid," write what you were afraid of. "I was afraid my daughter had been in an accident," for example.

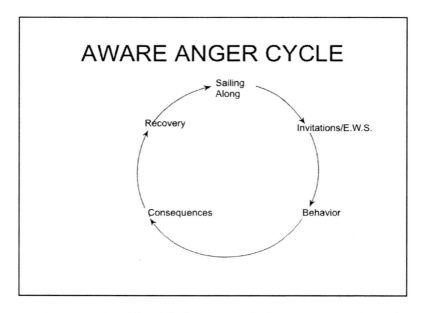

Once you've identified your underlying emotion(s), take a look at your physical reaction(s). Try to remember how you physically felt. Sometimes drawing a little stick figure of yourself may help. Did your eyes bug out? Did your voice quaver? Did your scalp get hot, your face get red, your hands shake, your palms get clammy?

Now you are ready to take a look at what options you may have had instead of going to anger. If you were hurt, you could have cried or said, "I am feeling hurt."

You may realize that you are often in this situation. So, before it happens again, you may be able to tell your son, husband, mother, father, wife, etc., "next time this happens, next time I feel this way when we're having a discussion, I'm going to take a 5-minute break and then come back." This is a common solution and one that works well if everyone involved knows ahead of time.

I would encourage you to do this exercise with other scenarios. When you look back at the underlying feelings, you will learn a lot about yourself and about the real reason you reacted in the way that you did. You may learn that, despite a reputation for being tough and flying off the handle, you are really quite sensitive and get your feelings hurt easily. Anger could be your way of hiding this vulnerable side of you. Some of us use anger to get people away from us. Everyone involved is then focused on the behaviors rather than the real issue at hand. In this way, anger is a very effective avoidance tool.

Conversely, you may be shocked to realize that while you are thought of as an amiable person, a "team-player" as it were, you are uncomfortable with confrontation and therefore holding your anger inside. This can result in emotional eating or drinking at the least and some more serious health problems at most. Wherever you find yourself, you'll now have the tools to move forward.

TAKE A BATH AND THINK ABOUT IT!

SECTION 4

Redefining the Word "Help"

"Real Power is Measured by How Much
You Can Let Things Be."

Thoreau

Space Invaders

Stop Doing the Laundry

Geri was a single mother whose 17-year-old son had been truant for most of his high school career. The judge gave her the choice between getting a certificate from my workshop or paying a significant fine. At the time, I was conducting workshops in my role as a Behavior Resource Specialist for the alternative programs. Most of the parents in my classes had students in an alternative setting but there were plenty who ended up there because their child was truant from other schools in the district. Geri, like many other parents, chose to come to the workshop in lieu of paying a fine.

A sinewy little stick of a woman, she blew into the room that first night, eyes wide and round like her hair was on fire. At first I thought someone was chasing her. She found a seat while vociferously letting the rest of the group know that she did not want to be there at all. There was no help for her son; she was waiting for his 18th birthday when the school officials would stop plaguing her about his attendance which she had no control over. It was a hopeless cause. She didn't understand why they couldn't see that.

The first assignment I give to parents, at the end of our first session, is to cease doing their kid's laundry. It's an admittedly simple assignment, although often difficult to implement. The cultural assumption has been that the more I do for my kid, the better parent I am. Truthfully however, the reverse is true: less is more. "Do less," I tell parents. "Be present more."

At the conclusion of Geri's first session, upon hearing the assignment, her outrage was uncontainable. "I did not come here to teach my kid how to do laundry. I came here so he'd go to school!"

"Right," I agreed.

"I cook his meals and clean his room and do his laundry; all I ask of him is that he go to school. That's it! That's all he has to concentrate on!"

This is where Dr. Phil's common response comes in handy. "So, how's that working for you?" I ask. And I ask kindly. I think of myself as a kind of mirror in these situations, a gentle reflection on reality, on what *is* as opposed to what people perceive.

Geri was in tatters trying so hard to do what was right for her son. I understand this. I still have the tendency to give unsolicited input to my grown kids. Because of years of practice, I can usually stop myself, realizing they are entitled to their journey. I played myself out early on in so many ways, expended so much of my good energy on talking, on giving "good" advice. If I told you how many times I've participated in this exercise in futility it would sound like I was whining.

To her credit, Geri was willing to trust the process. I agreed to her request that she be able to tell her son that *I* would not allow her to wash his clothes because she did not think she was strong enough to resist his opposition.

She returned the second week to convey her shock as she watched her son throw a tantrum like a two-year-old upon hearing that he'd be responsible for his own clothes. Not surprising really as he'd not ever been expected to do anything at home. Geri's self-imposed guilt for being a single parent and recovering addict affected her outlook profoundly. She was judged by her mother and, she felt, by all of society because she failed in getting him to go to school. "He actually stomped his feet on the ground and punched the air with his fists." This object lesson helped the group understand how scary it can be for a kid to do for himself when he's not had practice. We are all familiar on some level with the fear of failure. Further discussion on developmental stages opened Geri's eyes to hopeful possibilities for both her and her son.

Geri stuck to her guns though and followed through with her promise to teach him how to operate the machine if he needed help. By the third week, she beamed as she told me and the other parents, "He not only does his laundry, he does mine as well." It was the beginning of her son's realization that he could do more than just play video games. Geri completed the workshop where she filled her parenting bag with more tools and, with the help of a diligent school employee, saw her son complete high school.

Geri was a prime example of what I like to call "Space Invaders." These are people who are in the personal space of others; parents are especially adept at this form of invasiveness, always with the best of intentions.

Resonance imaging shows us how our own personal energy field extends past the perimeter of our flesh and blood. We, as a human society, are learning more and more about the earth's magnetic fields and we are now able to use that knowledge to connect with people miles away, like through the internet. Through the newer field of quantum physics, we are realizing that space as we've thought of it doesn't really exist. There's always something happening on a molecular level both in and around us. In much the same way, we are discovering and learning to work rightly within our own magnetic fields, that space right around our bodies which still contains our energy, what is known in the Eastern world as our chi. Here in the West, we refer to it as our spirit.

We were each born with a body but also with an area that extends out into the world around us. Sociologists have long recognized this as "personal space." This space is about 18 inches from our bodies. All of us are entitled to our space. We experience discomfort when people, other than ourselves, are in this space uninvited. Hugs, kisses, intimate chats, these we don't readily accept from the guy next to us on the bus. These are "invitation only" acts.

As parents, what we hope for is to be invited into the space of our children especially when they need us. However, if we are constantly in this space uninvited, then all of the kid's energy is spent on getting us out—just like we do with anyone who is invading our own personal space.

Whether chi or energy or spirit or personal space, whatever you choose to call it, we can clearly see that there is a part of us that is, as Emily Dickinson says, "Invisible as Music, but positive as sound." Some children really love to share their space with their parents often. Others prefer to keep a bit of distance. Being invited in is a privilege, a golden moment for parents.

Letting Go

The Hardest Thing I've Ever Had To Do

My daughter is a powerful woman who, like many of us as young women, had not yet realized her own strength of will and therefore used her own power against herself instead of in her favor. You see, my precious, beautiful, strong, thoughtful, devoted, wouldn't-hurt-a-fly, sweetheart of a girl, was in an emotionally abusive relationship with someone who could see none of those qualities. When the pain became unbearable, she would talk to me about it for hours either in person or on the phone and cry and tell me stories I did not want to hear.

I thought I was helping. I thought as her mother it was my duty to listen at all hours of the night, and to offer urgent advice (read: tell her what to do) which in the moment she seemed to heed and understand. Yet, in the morning on my way to work, I'd drive by her house and see his car there yet again. My stomach was in knots. Every time I drove by, I felt like throwing up. I told my wise and trusted friend, Patricia, that I just wasn't sure what else I could do. Pat loved me and she loved my daughter and knew us well.

"I'd suggest you take another route to work," Pat said kindly and calmly.

I was stunned and, I admit, a little pissed. "What?!"

"How old is she, Terri?" She remained calm.

"Twenty-one," I said but as I said it I realized that I didn't believe it. In my mind she was still 11 and lost. Fortunately, I was learning to recognize my tendency toward defensive anger as an old companion pointing me toward truth. So, I was able to calm down and listen.

"She's an adult and she's making adult choices."

"I know," I conceded. "But, she's making *terrible* choices!"

"And, whose behavior can you control in this situation?"

We both knew the answer to that rhetorical question.

I still cared and cared fiercely but I accepted that she was the only one who could get herself out of this situation. Nothing illegal was happening so there was no leverage there. All of my stomachaches and headaches and wanting it to be different would not change a thing. I did not come to this realization easily. My head was a bloody mess from having banged it up against this same wall over and over and over again. This truth did, in fact, lead to my taking another route to work and getting on with my day without having to take medication for a splitting head.

As I eased back from the situation, I began to see a pattern that I couldn't see when I was so close. I saw that when my daughter became desperately unhappy and felt up against the wall, she would come to me. She would cry, I would console and she'd feel better. With the pressure off, she went right back to her old ways. It was the equivalent of picking up a drunk relative from the lawn night after night, cleaning them up and tucking them neatly into bed instead of leaving them out there to wake up with the consequences of their actions. Obviously, the latter is the most promising avenue to change while at the same time being the scariest.

So, I devised a plan. I gave my daughter three phone numbers. The first was the number of a friend who had, as a young woman, gone through a cycle of abusive relationships before she finally learned how to free herself. The second was the number of a friend who had suffered from depression and anxiety for most of her life and had finally learned to manage her condition and live joyfully. The third was the number of a counselor who was willing to see my daughter and who thought she could help.

When I gave her these three numbers, I said, "I will be here for you but I will not talk to you about this relationship anymore because I see it does you no good. If you feel you need to talk, please use one or all of these numbers. They are expecting you to call and more than happy to offer help."

I could only do this after I'd gotten to the end of myself. I had not been in an abusive relationship. I had not been depressed. I was not a mental health professional. I could only do this after I reasoned that if she had been physically sick and I had tried unsuccessfully over and over to cure her, I would then take her to the doctor. I could only do this after I'd realized that while I loved that she came to me and I liked thinking I was a help, there was nothing else I could do to *truly* help her.

It took about two weeks before she came to our house one night and just burst out crying. I was already in bed. She lay down beside me and I held her as she sobbed. I knew what it was about even though she was crying too hard to speak. When she finally was able to speak, she launched into the most recent horror with the boyfriend but as soon as she said his name I interrupted.

"Sweetheart, I told you that I would not talk with you about this again. Do you still have those 3 numbers?"

She nodded her head yes as her eyes registered disbelief. "Have you used them?"

She shook her head.

This was one of the hardest things I've ever done, but also one of the most effective both for her and for myself. I was able to be sympathetic and caring and *truly* helpful. She tested me more than once on this ultimatum. I was able to stick to it only through the support of my friend, and eventually, my daughter did seek help.

There are whole books and seminars and classes and philosophies created around the topic of giving our loved ones their own space in a much broader sense. In our society we sometimes refer to this as "letting go." Obviously we never let go of our children altogether. But it is helpful to be able to understand the need for space and when it is appropriate to back away in certain situations. These situations will differ with your child's age and developmental stage.

With each letting go, there comes a trust that your child is going to be okay without you. Sometimes they will need help and the best help will not necessarily come from you. Note that if your identity as a person is not intact, you probably don't really want your child to be okay without you, to need someone else besides you, or to be independent of you. In this case, perhaps a visit back to Stage 5 and the Identity Crisis, on your own behalf, would be useful.

Building from early childhood, on smaller to larger instances, there eventually comes a point when your son or daughter will *want* but not necessarily *need* you. This is the Golden Moment of parenting. My mentor, Joyce, introduced this concept to me as I stewed and fretted about some of the decisions my adult children were making. I was still trying to "help them" by offering advice when it wasn't wanted and hovering because I assumed I knew better than they did about themselves. "Let go," Joyce said to me. "And wait to be invited back into their lives."

As I've said before, my older kids got the short end of the stick; I came to these realizations later rather than sooner in their lives. My daughter helped me so much with this concept. She, more than any of my children, taught me the ability to love while being healthily detached. She brought to light a life-changing truth and helped me to accept it: my behavior is the only behavior I will ever be able to control.

So, the answer to, "When do I let go?" is now. Today. Every chance you get. Because the sooner you begin this process in small incremental steps, the sooner your child will be able to stand on his or her own two feet. Only then can you can help them to walk and then run and then soar.

Momism

Mommy, Dearest

In his 1976 book titled, *Momism*, the sociologist Hans Sebald argues that there is a "type of mother who is an expert in personality assassination. Her art of ambush resides and specializes in playing the "good" mother, and she goes about her stealthy business with impunity and, indeed, social reward." While I have great respect for Hans Sebald and do see his point, there are a couple of things I would like to point out. For one, Sebald's assertion targets only one parent, the mother. Also, he seems to be laying blame without much compassion for any possible lack of development on her part. This makes her appear purposeful in her bent as opposed to unknowing. However, Sebald recognized the beginnings of a phenomenon in our culture which ultimately became known in the '90's as the "Soccer Mom."

Soccer Moms are portrayed, in essence, as overburdened women who clearly put their children's needs before their own. They are lauded and proud of their exhausting schedules and lack of self-care. There's a lot more to the concept but there is one particular aspect I'd like to focus on, the part that Sebald didn't account for: the needs of the parent as a person.

This is what I believe to be the most insidious aspect of parenting in our current culture. The expectation that a child is more important than the adult, or that any one person should take precedence in the family, is caustic on many levels. We could talk for books (and many have) about the resulting "me" generation, the super-busyness of many American families, and about consumer costs and ecological effects. But I'd like to focus on a shift in perspective that changes everything: helping parents to see that parenting is a *role*, and not an *identity*. I know. Stunning, right?

I incur more ire from this concept than probably any other. So, let's slow down here and take a careful look. We can clearly see from our brief look at Erikson's Life Stages of Development that everyone is in their own "stuff." We are all, at any point in time in our lives, experiencing crisis. We make a "bajillion" decisions a day because we get a "bajillion" invitations to respond. "So, Terri, how can I make the right decisions for myself while at the same time ensuring that my kid is cared for?" Simple: as much as possible, let your child make decisions for her own life. In Erikson's Life Stages, we see that beginning in the Toddler stage, we begin to recognize our own autonomy. The "personality assassination" comes when a parent does not allow the child to hold sway in her own life, beginning with minute and low-cost decisions. Hat or cap? Gloves or mittens? Juice or milk? This is why I so appreciate the ever popular *Love & Logic®* approach to this stage of development and recommend it highly to parents of young children.

In this way you can watch as your child evolves safely into the person they truly are. You can practice allowing them to express their own style, their own tastes, their own likes and dislikes. You can practice opening your heart and loving your child even if you are a Macintosh family and, God forbid, she chooses a PC.

However, what gets in the way of allowing your child to take part in her own life, the fear of allowing her choices, is your own stuff. Ask yourself: "Where does this come from?" Usually, it stems from trying so hard to be a good parent and to help the kids "get it right." *You* have to Get. It. Right! And here is where I part from Sebald's assessment.

The underlying reason for any parent's "mistakes" is from a firmly held, societally-supported belief that they *must* get this "right." The very existence of another soul rests on their getting it right, for Pete's sake!

For instance, one of my clients, a brilliant single mother of a bubbly nine-year old, was worried to death about her daughter's messy habits hurting her career prospects. Really? She's *nine*. Will the mud on her nine-year old feet really keep her from being a CEO in 20 years? You can see, though, how the pressure of parenting can really take us captive into the future and have us miss the present altogether.

To delve into this question of "getting it right" is one of the most eye-opening aspects of this whole process. You can probably see that you have, somewhere along the line, adopted a view of parental "right" and "wrong" and that many times this view is not your own. Some of you see that you've taken on your own parents' dictums while readily admitting that this course provided little for your own developmental growth. Some of you have well-meaning friends or family looking over your shoulders "helping" you out with suggestions that do not resonate with you at all or, interestingly enough, spewing advice that so far hasn't helped the spewers themselves.

Once we see that we all have our own lives and that the only person we are 100% guaranteed to live with throughout this life is ourselves, then we can begin to put right our own course. We can begin to help our children become independent of us and continue on with our own lives seeing parenting as a temporary job resulting in a permanent relationship. We will always love our children, be involved in their lives, and continue to be Mom and Dad even to adults. But parenting has a very definite purpose: as we shepherd our children, allowing them to expand into maturity, we have the opportunity to expand and grow as well.

Momism basically describes my early years as a parent. My kids played soccer, were in band, on the dance team, ran track, played tennis and baseball and football and wrestled and took music lessons. My husband and I both worked and at one point agreed to never be at the same event unless it was a monumental one. We just didn't have the time to spare. One of us needed to be home starting dinner and homework with the rest of the brood. This doesn't even cover the time I spent with cooking, family and school events, medical appointments, church commitments, or the planning and paperwork for each of these.

But, for all of my perceived faults, I was dutiful and felt personally responsible for the happiness of everyone in the house. I was taught it. I am a good student to the degree that I carried it over into my teaching career. You can imagine how that worked out. Trying to be emotionally, if not personally, responsible for students who walked into my classroom from every conceivable lifestyle and situation. And we wonder about teacher burnout! As parents we aren't allowed to burnout. We can't quit. Or can we? Think about alcohol, caffeine, tobacco, TV, medicines that numb (both legal and illegal), overeating, staying busy, busy, busy. "Getting it right" comes with a very high price.

I have a dear friend who is one of the most conscientious people I know. She's responsible and caring, has an important job dealing with people's very lives. Her children depend on her, her staff depends on her, her husband depends on her, her friends depend on her, her children's teammates and coaches depend on her. She's a very capable woman. Capable and exhausted as even when her body is resting, her mind is on the hamster wheel. She is taking care of everyone but herself. Sound familiar?

One night we were in her family's kitchen which is a hubbub of delightful activity in the after-school evenings. Her 13-year-old daughter thought it would be fun to make a pie from a simple mix found in the pantry. I sat back and watched as her mother (just home from work and scrambling to get supper ready) dutifully "helped" her. Having never made a pie before, the girl was curious and exuberant and, understandably, a bit unsure of herself. It was the perfect opportunity for her to gain confidence, to gain a sense of self-efficacy. Her mother, although busy with her own cooking, could not keep her hands off of the pie project. Instead of simply explaining questions asked (and there were many at first), she "helped" her daughter, explaining while doing the task as the girl stood back watching.

Two things jumped out at me in this scenario. First, the opportunity to put a brick in the wall of self-esteem was missed. Second, had my friend simply answered questions as she cooked, she would have expended less physical and much less mental energy. But, in an attempt to help her daughter get it right, and for her to feel like she was getting it right as a parent, a less than perfect pie was not in the mix.

I thought again of the concept of self-esteem and how it cannot be taught. Thus, the operative word, "self." We can't convince people of their beauty, neither inside beauty nor outside beauty. Just look at the rash of debilitating habits and destructive neuroses amongst supermodels, for instance. Yet the world sees them as exemplars of beauty. In the same way, we cannot convince others of their abilities. They must *experience* their capabilities for themselves. No amount of praise can take the place of a true sense of accomplishment.

It seems a small thing, right? We say we're so busy and it is true. But, in my estimation, many of us are busy doing what others could do for themselves.

Think of it this way: Can you exercise for your child? "Oh, honey, by the way, I ran three miles today for you so you should be feeling really good. Go ahead and have that extra slice of pizza." Or "Sweetie, I did your homework so you'll be able to pass that algebra test with no problem."

Can you just hear the insanity of this line of thinking?

Yet, it seems to permeate our parental psyches. We really, really want to save our children so we give them advice, we do their homework, do their chores, over-parent when what would be most helpful is overseeing *their* development.

Your involvement with your children does not lessen as they develop but it does change. Your heart will always be with them. Your hands, however, become less and less needed. Your challenge then as a parent is to keep your heart engaged while incrementally handing over the reins of your child's life to the rightful owner. This requires trust. In most cases, adults will have to deal with their own trust issues in order to complete the transfer. For some this requires a trust in the process, or in your child, in your own intuition, in the input of a wise friend, in God, or in all of the above. This is a significant change in direction for most of us.

The earlier you understand the importance of trading trust for worry, the better off you'll be. The good news is that it is definitely not too late.

Many of us were taught, not so much with words but by shining example, that worrying is synonymous with caring. If we constantly feel bad for someone then we are somehow helping them. My 82-year old mother still expresses her love and concern for me by saying, "I worry about your health, your car, your job, your kids, etc."

"Mom," I've learned to say, "please send me good thoughts instead of worrying. Think of my life as you'd like it to be."

But Mom, like many of us, believes she must feel bad for someone in order to care about them. Ultimately your feeling bad doesn't help. Your feeling bad will not affect change. Your taking action will.

We don't have to feel bad in order to be good people. We don't have to be worried about our kids in order to be effective parents. Turn would-be worry into positive action. Worry doesn't add a single thing to our lives. Ask yourself instead, "What can I *do* about it? Equally as important is, "What is it that I *cannot* do in this situation?"

I once heard a pastor speaking about how worry and faith don't live in the same world. He said something that changed me. "Stop preparing for the worst thing to happen to your kid. You *can't* prepare for it. So stop trying." For a person who used to get up at night to see if my kids were breathing (not babies, *kids*), this was like a lightning bolt to the head. For years, I'd imagined the worst when my teenagers walked out the door at night. It was torture. But it was what I knew to do. Thankfully, his words helped me begin to see the futility of the exercise.

Bottom Line

As soon as you realize that your child is in control of her choices, you can begin to unclench your fists. And when you do, you see that there is nothing there but air, no tether to another's will. Your hand will then be open to help. You will no longer live with the illusion that you control another's behavior and you will be free to get on with making choices about your own life and how to better respond to the choices of all of your significant others.

In her wonderful book, *Loving What Is*, Byron Katie contends that all of our suffering is caused by confusion. When I read this, I realized that this concept of suffering is always related to the question of who is in control. Not who *should be* but who is. The only person's behavior that we can control is our own. As soon as we realize this truth, we are on the road to freedom.

Ask Yourself

What is it I am hoping to improve about my life? Why am I in this situation? How did I get here? What are the things I can do to cause change? What are the things I cannot do?

Try This

Get a pencil and paper. Take a breath deep enough for you to hear and let it out slowly. Think about the answers to these questions. Take your time. Write them down as if no one will ever see them. If it'll help you be honest, tear up the answers once you've seen them.

Hopefully, you will realize that no matter who you've given credit or blame to for your current situation, you did and always will have some choice in the way you handle the matter.

As you continue through this book, you will become much clearer on the importance of taking responsibility for your own life and for your own style of parenting. Basically, it's the difference in living life as a victim or a victor and passing this along to your children. And, just like the Hokey-Pokey, "that's what it's all about!"

TAKE A BATH, YEAH!

SECTION 5

Tools

"Everything that irritates us about others can
lead us to an understanding of ourselves."

Carl Jung

Whose Life Is It, Anyway?

Going Into the Closet

When my daughter was in eighth grade she had trouble fitting in with the popular group. This gaggle of middle school girls knew there were definite "ins" and definite "outs." To be a part of the "in" circle, the "outs" had to be clearly identified and kept at bay. This is typical behavior in those who don't yet have a developed sense of self.

My daughter has always been full of vibrant energy, creativity and color. As a child, she used her Barbie dolls to explore and express all of these personal attributes. The clothes, the hair, the furniture, the houses, the career choices, the protocol, the manners, she played with all of it like the Goddess of Life and it was a joy to behold. So it was especially disturbing to me to find that she had taken Barbie into the closet. When I questioned her about this she was ashamed but at the same time explained quite convincingly that she didn't want one of her friends to happen upon her playing with Barbie dolls and have it get back to school.

Remember how I said at the beginning of this book that I had a big heart but a low skill set? Keep that in mind. I, of course, went into the old, "You must be who you are." "You won't remember these girls in five years." "You can't let others dictate your behavior or you'll never stop." "This is just plain silly and frankly I thought you were made of better stuff." I know! I KNOW! I'm cringing with you.

Fortunately, I was taking a Developmental Child Psych class that term and it became increasingly clear to me that her peers, at age 12, were just as important to her as mine were to me at age 32. So, when I came home one day and found her in the same closet crying because one of the mean girls had gotten to her that day at school, I was able to get into the closet with her (it was a roomy closet). And, more importantly, I didn't talk. I rocked her while she sobbed and sobbed and tried to tell me all about it. I held her and I held my tongue and I was so grateful that I had finally learned to do both.

Erikson helps us to realize that we are all on some page of our human experience. We may have turned the pages of childhood and adolescence in our own lives but we are very much in the throes of our current stage of development. If nothing else, this understanding will lead to a more humble approach. Yes, you've had more life experiences and seen more but, ultimately, we're all traveling together here.

Respect for the developmental stage, no matter what age, is always helpful. Picture an opening flower as the example of the child's brain. We can only accept and understand information that our brain is ready to receive. This helps to explain why a very bright first grader, for instance, cannot understand the concept of algebra. The brain hasn't opened up that far. Therefore, trying to cram in that information is a futile exercise.

So, when we deal with our kids, we can come from a place of respect for their current position in life. Also, given our understanding of our own position, we are less likely to say things like, "grow up and get over it."

The previous chapters have been filled with information for you to ponder. Now it is time for action. Even if your kids are of an age to dress themselves, drive themselves, live on their own or otherwise mind their own business, you can still expend lots of energy thinking about what they *should* be doing.

Let's look at a few strategies that can actually help in relieving you of the burden of their lives. It's too much for you to carry, really it is. You may lay it down and begin to live your own life while you share rightfully in your child's.

Ask, Don't Tell

Once I asked a boy dressed in all black why he was at school. I was addressing another teacher's class and this young man made it clear that he would rather be doing anything besides listening to me. He was new to the group and unlike the other students had no history with me.

"I don't have no choice." He looked away from me in disgust from beneath his dark bangs.

"You have no choice?"

The rest of the class, very familiar by now with this line of questioning, averted their eyes or smiled slightly.

"I'm here," he said with a smirk, "because my mom made me come."

"Your mom *made* you come?"

"Phh-yueah. Otherwise I wouldn't be here. That's for sure."

I creased my brow. "How tall is your mom?"

Clearly this wasn't a question he expected. He took his chair from his backward-leaning position down to all fours to look at me squarely. "She's 5'2".

"And, how tall are you?"

"6'2"."

"And, so, how did your mom make you come when you are obviously so much bigger than she is? Did she stuff you into the car and force you into the classroom once you got here?" I leaned in trying to understand.

He rolled his eyes as if talking to a moron. "She told me if I didn't come to school, I'd hafta move out."

"So, it looks to me like you made a choice to come to school."

"Uh-no. I just told you that she's gonna kick me out if I don't come."

"But I know lots of people whose parents say the same thing to them and they aren't here. They made the choice not to come to school anyway."

Now it was his turn to crinkle his brow.

I continued. "What I mean is that you made a choice to keep a roof over your head, right?"

He hesitated, then nodded.

"Which I think is very smart," I said as I smiled in approval.

Asking questions is the best way to help your child begin to de-victimize himself. This student went from being a victim to seeing that he actually did have a choice in the matter. He wasn't comfortable with this as many people aren't. They'd much rather blame their discontent on someone else. But if someone at home were asking him questions based on his very real freedom of choice, rather than telling him what to do, he'd soon realize his own personal power could be used to better his life.

I once heard a renowned psychologist say while being interviewed about his new book, that all unsolicited advice is self-serving. I was as shocked as the interviewer by this assertion. "All?" She asked.

"All," he affirmed. His claim was that we give people advice most of the time because it makes *us* feel better. We care about our loved ones so when they are in emotional turmoil, we assuage our own empathetic churnings by offering help. This is where redefining the word "help" comes in handy.

He went on to say that if people aren't asking questions, they are not yet ready for answers. Therefore, our attempts to give them counsel, as wise as that counsel may be, is futile and often frustrating for all parties.

When I heard this I was still teaching. A light went off in my head that forever changed the course of my methodology. What I needed to do was to get my students to ask questions, to engage them cognitively everyday in their own behaviors, actions and choices.

I began to use this in the classroom and at home and with most people I encountered. Having grown up in a family where, "what you need to do is . . . ," was an oft spoken phrase, this was such a relief. It did take practice and still does.

I began to teach this way using something I learned from my dad, a tugboat captain. Tugboats are meant to push or pull other vessels. They have really big engines that take up the bulk of space on a tug. They can be very helpful to others. Interestingly enough, the ropes that connect these little helpful powerhouses to the bigger vessels, must come from those big vessels themselves. The tug sits there bobbing in the harbor waiting patiently for a line. The ship must *want* to get through an obstacle in order to receive help from the tug. In the same way, what you know is only valuable to those who see the value in it.

If a fancy, big, beautiful ship needs to get through the locks of the Panama Canal, for instance, this ship must be pulled to the other side by a tugboat. If the ship does not throw lines down to the tug, then it sits there in all of its glorious potential never able to get to the high seas for which it was made.

What you want your child to do is to begin to ask questions of you, to throw you a line so you can give them answers that can help them realize their potential. It's helpful then to ask yourself when dealing with your kid, "Have I asked a question?" or "Have I been asked a question?" Because, otherwise, they are probably not listening.

Majoring on the Minors

Years ago there was a family in my church, a mom and dad and 3 lovely daughters. The mom was pleasant and conscientious and the girls were nice, decent and, on the whole, far above average. I was newly married to the Youth Pastor, which gave me a window on lots of parenting styles and their results. So, I asked this particular mother what she did to have such a great outcome with her kids and her answer has been a theme of mine ever since.

"Don't major on the minors," she told me almost glibly.

"What does that mean?"

"It means that I know my fourteen year old daughter wears too much make-up and that my middle girl sometimes wears her skirts too short."

I smiled knowingly because there were some in our congregation who believed these things to be true and, because her husband was a church leader, judged her accordingly.

She returned my smile and went on. "Contrary to what some believe, these choices are not immoral ones so I leave them alone. I think of myself as a flour sifter. It's only the big things that won't get through."

Most people believe that it's a good idea to let people make their own choices. The scary part for the parents I sometimes deal with is that their kids have made poor, and often horrific, choices for themselves. Their records are not that good when it comes to outcome-based thinking.

This is why it is best to begin giving them choices early on. When they're small, the consequence of a poor choice is small. As they age, the consequences have much more of an impact on their lives.

It's helpful to remember that you really cannot control another person's behavior. You can, however, give them choices based on your own predetermined actions. It's also helpful to understand that a choice that does not match with your own personal preference does not necessarily constitute a "wrong" choice.

It Always Takes Two to Argue

Graciella came into my workshop because her 15-year old daughter had been suspended for skipping class, as was her habit.

"I tell her to go to school, her father promises her anything she wants, but it always ends up in a shouting match. She does what she wants," Graciella said quietly and with much sadness. "I have no control over where she goes or who she sees or what she does."

"Is this true?" As I asked this, Graciella kept her eyes on the flat surface of the conference table and nodded. "You have *no* power?"

This time, she lifted her chin to look at me questioningly.

I questioned her again, "Are you sure?"

Now she was able to see my smile. She smiled slightly for the first time that evening. After all of the information, the stories of other parents, the testimonies of change, for the first time she smiled with the hope that what she had believed up to this point may not be true.

"If school is not important to her and what you want for her is not important, then what is important to her?"

"Her friends. Her clothes. Her nails. Her cell phone?" At this the other parents smiled and laughed in recognition. Graciella giggled shyly.

Because we had already gone over the Psychosocial Stages of Development, Graciella knew that her daughter was in the adolescent stage and that it was normal for her friends to be important to her. This was what was right with the picture. It was important to her daughter that her friends saw her look her best, that she make a good impression. Once Graciella realized that there is power in the purse strings, she was able to realize that she did not have to pay for her daughter's regularly scheduled nail fills, her mall visits, nor her blingy cell phone. These were choices she had made and she could "unchoose" to make them. She'd need support to follow through, but the sheer realization that she was not powerless was startling.

The beginning of this change at home was not arguing with her daughter. I encouraged her to create an alliance with her husband based on this newly discovered knowledge and there was to be absolutely no arguing whatsoever.

"Arguing makes you equals."

I learned this truth long ago from Harper Lee. *To Kill a Mockingbird* is my favorite book of all time; I have taught it for years to both high school and college students. This story of a small town lawyer and his two children seems to transcend age and culture in its humanness.

There's one scene in the book where Scout, the younger of the two children, is trying to get her big brother, Jem, to fight with her. Jem has gotten into the recent habit of agreeing with their father and taking a more adult view of things, which disturbs Scout greatly as she and Jem have been constant allies against their father since she's been alive. Scout knows full well that Jem, if riled to anger, can hurt her with words and worse, yet she happily antagonizes him to violence against her. Why?

It's because Socrates and those other ancients crafted the art of argument as a method of reasoning between two intellectual equals. In other words, we argue with those who share an equality with us. Scout knew that if she could get Jem to argue with her, to lose his temper, no matter what the consequences, she would have won. He would still be on her level after all and not have gone off irretrievably into the unknown and really scary world of adult reason.

This was so helpful to me in realizing why my nine-year old son would do and say things on purpose to make me mad. He knew the outcome and yet he would hit his brother in front of me or sass me right to my face. He did not *know* so much as he *felt* that if I lost my temper, which I did, that he still had some control over the situation.

It always takes two to argue. If you can see this and choose not to engage, then there will be no arguing between you and your child. It's just that simple.

The truth is that you as the adult have the power. There can be no power struggle unless you do not fully realize this truth. You are the provider. It is your household.

So, as much as possible, ignore the behaviors you don't want and respect with affirmation and trust, the behaviors you do want. This is a good practice for both you and your child.

What this all boils down to, in essence, is that old, old, ancient adage we've heard forever: *action speaks louder than words.* What we do speaks volumes in comparison to what we say and no one knows this better than our children.

Night Time is the Right Time

Our girls shared a small room, as did the two little boys so reading to them at bedtime was easy. I read to the girls and Wayne typically read to the boys. It strengthened our bond. Research has shown that all of us are more vulnerable when we are tired. Being with your kids at night allows a relaxed atmosphere for soft conversation. For me, that time meant I had to stop doing whatever was so important and go sit for thirty minutes. For the girls, it was a time to relax, get lost in the world of young, female pioneers or *Anne of Green Gables*, and feel the security of an adult in the room. Wayne ended his time with the boys by singing to each of them their own special song each night.

Recently I was given a small wall plaque which reads, "Don't just do something, sit there." Sitting with the kids during these nighttime rituals was a practice in doing just that. It wasn't that I did nothing, per se, but I learned to allow special moments to unfold and to look for them. Eventually I learned not to try to fix things during this time but to offer reassurance and, more importantly, non-alarm in the face of situations that worried or tried them. It was during these nightly moments together that I was able to look at each child, to actually watch their faces and expressions as they spoke or asked a question. I began to get a glimpse into their way of being, into their spirits as it were.

For instance, after I finished reading a Janette Oke story about the young pioneer woman who had to marry a man she initially didn't love, one of the girls said with some disdain, "I could never do that! She didn't even know him!" The other two began to counter with their own feelings on the situation, "he was nice, he was honest, he was kind, what else could she do, etc." It gave me a chance to hear their feelings and it gave them a chance to ruminate on what they deemed important.

Later, I read about a woman who set her alarm for 12:58 every Friday night. She went into the kitchen for a glass of water as her daughter, who stayed up to watch the late movie, was headed off to bed. Her daughter, a busy teenager, had grown increasingly distant and uncommunicative. The simple off-handed question of "How was the movie?" led to many discussions which otherwise would never have happened. She credits this to the vulnerability that being tired and relaxed can bring. Now a grandmother, she looks back on these conversations as some of the sweetest times in her role as a parent.

Driving Lessons

The door slammed behind him as he breezed through the den, not saying a word, lips in a tight line, eyes straight ahead. Had he been a drinking man, he would have headed straight for the Scotch. As it was, he heavy-stepped to his study, grabbed the newest issue of the *New Yorker* and headed for the bathroom. I'm almost sure he didn't draw a breath until he was seated.

She followed, door slamming behind her timid, unsure step. Her eyes were cast down.

"How'd it go?" I ventured.

She didn't look at me. "It was okay," she quavered on her way to her room, her straight, black hair swinging choppily with each step.

I should have been used to the scenario. But, I was always hopeful that they would one day walk through the door arm in arm, my husband and my daughter. She would beam. He would look at me with eyes that said, "This was the day!" Obviously, *this* was not that day.

When he finally came out of the bathroom, I was in the kitchen loading the dishwasher. I let him stand there leaning against the counter behind me silently waiting for me to look at him. I turned with a warm plate in my hand to ease the chill.

At my questioning look he shrugged, "Some people just can't do it." He continued in helpless persistence, "They can't, they just can't. It doesn't mean she's a bad person."

The words of Professor Thompson, my gray-haired, bike-riding, lover of life psychology professor, rang in my head, "Research has shown us that if your brain is fairly normal and you hear the information enough, you will eventually get it. Sometimes, it's just like a light going off. Don't drop the class just yet, give it some time." I chose to believe her and ended up with an A in a class that initially terrified me.

I remembered this as my husband stood there telling me my daughter would never be able to drive. "No," I countered. "She just may take more time than most."

So, I took over the driving lessons and what I began to realize is that people drive just as they live. All of my kids approached driving just like they approached life. Some were tense, some were stubborn, some were receptive, some were confident, some were over-confident, some were petrified and wanted to be left alone, and some took longer than others to realize their foot was actually on the gas instead of the brake.

I began to look at all people in light of the way they drove. My husband was always in a hurry, rarely aware of what was going on around him yet hurling headlong into traffic. I was always tense and afraid I was going to run over something or someone.

Over the years, this premise that people drive as they live has continued to be borne out in my observations of friends and relatives. Some are careful, some are hesitant, some are bold. So, I tell you this in light of the upcoming event, the almost inevitable occasion of teaching your child to drive. Watch. Listen. Learn. Even when they are adults, ask them to take you to the store, or for a drive in the country. You'll learn as much as just about any conversation can tell you about their approach to life at that moment in time.

Bottom Line

You can probably see that the implementation of these tools will require some patience and persistence on your part. When you are tired, these tasks will seem insurmountable. The hope is that you will begin to value your time and to take care of yourself so you can in turn take care of your child. Being kind to your child ultimately will not happen unless you are first kind to yourself. Maya Angelou encourages us: "Do the best you can until you know better. Then when you know better, do better."

Ask Yourself

How many hours of sleep do I get? Is it enough? What could I do to change this? Am I acting respectfully toward my child? Is my tone kind, empathetic? And, most importantly, do I do what I say I will do?

Try This

Albert Einstein said that imagination was more important than knowledge. Give yourself permission to write about the kind of parent you'd like to be. Imagine what that person would look like, sound like, act like. What would be this person's habits?

After you've written, give yourself permission to see yourself as this person. It is your best self. It is who you are already. Act as if you are this person and focus on sleep and rest for yourself so that your waking hours will be clear.

When you address your child this week, practice turning every would–be statement into a question. Example: "Go do your homework," becomes "Have you done your homework yet?"

HAVE YOU TAKEN YOUR BATH YET?

SECTION 6

Home, Hearth, Heart

"We're the ones we've been waiting for."

Adapted from Mohatma Ghandi

Stress Relief Through Structure

The sudden lurch into parenthood sent me to my knees. "Please don't let me mess them up," was my everyday prayer. I had a big heart and a gregarious spirit but all of the good attributes I could muster were tempered by a lack of knowledge when it came to the particular issues I was facing. Wayne and I, both before and after we were married, had spent lots of time with kids of all ages, which gave us confidence on one level. We had often commented on the ways of parents, making mental notes on what we would and would not do. This was very helpful. However, as with most parents, we had had no formal training, no manual, and now had to take into account six very different personalities, needs and wants.

The first weeks of our sudden family brought lots of hearts, hands and help to our door. Still we faced the daunting tasks of attaining school supplies and clothes, a larger house, a larger vehicle and feeding what seemed like "the five thousand."

John did not speak English, was not potty-trained and had already lost his front teeth to "bottle-mouth." He had never been taught to sit while eating. The girls did the best they could with him, usually following him, bowl and spoon in hand, as he tottered where he pleased. He had been put to bed most of his life by falling asleep in front of cartoon videos sometimes as late as 2 a.m. He reminded me of a little Buddha walking around in his diaper, a throng of trailing servants catering to his every need partly because he was so cute and partly because his temper, once unleashed, was not easily soothed.

Quy was (and still is) a boy with a sugar-sweet heart and a ready, easy laugh. You couldn't really fail kindergarten in those days but he had never made good grades, especially in conduct. This was due, in large part, to his enormous energy that could not be contained by his little body. He moved constantly, all day long until bedtime. As soon as he lay down, he fell asleep hard and fast but trying to optimally contain or occupy him was a challenge.

Chau was a cute little girl who spent her time charming adults. Smart and intense, she could do anything she set out to accomplish. She seemed to crave attention and approval and was often competing with other kids which didn't always end well.

Gabrielle had a major malocclusion that caused her bottom lip to very nearly touch her nose. It was hard for her to chew so eating was almost always a messy prospect. She had a severe hearing loss in one ear and was basically content to spend time in her own world unless and until she needed something or someone.

Oanh was serious and sad. She bore into me for comfort when she was not busy trying to continue to mother the other kids and sort out their needs. Having never experienced the freedom of childhood, she was uncomfortable with leisure time and was unsure as to how to join in with other kids who were playing even though she wanted to.

Tim was depressed. Although he was 18 and a legal adult, he was socially and emotionally very much a boy. Because of his age and place in the family, he had to be involved in legal proceedings that the other kids were often unaware of. There was a considerable disparity between who he was and what was expected of him. When at home, he slept as much as possible and was not always at his best when awake.

The clash of schedules, weariness, grief, and lack of space, all piled up into what seemed an insurmountable heap. I could hear the words of the old Johnny Mercer song ringing in my ears, "Something's gotta give!"

The move into a sizeable house with two bathrooms and a fenced yard was a start. No more falling all over each other like a litter of newborn puppies. The new house, coupled with the start of a brand new school year in a different school district, offered the formality of a new beginning. However, we still faced 8 different personal schedules, 168 meals a week and more loads of laundry than I could count.

Fortunately, my mother had taught me how to laugh and my mother-in-law had taught me how to make lists. Laughter and lists were the first two ladder rungs in our climb from chaos to order.

Structure, I have come to realize, was the first form of self-care that I practiced. There are so many unknowns in the day of a family whether large or small. Establishing at least some order allowed me to be able to focus on my family while maintaining a bit of personal well-being and peace of mind. Structure was my first step toward sanity.

Here is a list of some simple tools that helped me tremendously. As you read, some of you may feel overwhelmed. All of the time it takes to plan may seem like overkill; and, maybe it is for you. But, as with any event, it's the planning ahead that takes most of the time and thought. The actual activity takes much less time and goes much smoother if you've taken the time to prepare. Think of how much time goes into a wedding, for example, or a party or a graduation. Hours and hours go into planning events that sometimes take no more than minutes to execute.

That being said, please be sure to allow yourself a scale of progress. Even the best laid plans often end up a little left of center. Some of your plans may take a while to come to full implementation. As I tell my students, life will be much more enjoyable if you can just remember the "F" word: "Flexibility." Give your family a little wiggle room and give yourself some major credit for even the smallest move toward executing a plan.

Home

Calendar Central—Checking "the wall"

I t wasn't long before my lists grew from post–it size to desk pad-size to paper-size to notebook-size. So, I went one step larger and tacked a giant **dry-erase calendar** onto the kitchen wall. I was the only person allowed to write on the calendar and if the event wasn't written there, chances are it would be missed. All the field trips, music lessons, doctor or dental appointments, personal and professional appointments for everyone in the family, athletic events, birthday parties, and church outings were included on this surface. Everything was there and every eye could easily see it. Everyone was informed and conflicts were resolved sooner rather than later. The kids quickly gained the habit of checking "the wall" which kept me from feeling like I was constantly up against it! This was a lesson for them in working together as a family and helpful for me as it fostered their independence and curried personal responsibility. One of the best moves I ever made and a very easy place to start.

Menus and Meals—A "Bunch" With No Alice

It would've been nice to come home from work to find a hot meal on the stove or to have awakened in the morning to the smell of bacon and coffee on a carefully laid breakfast table. I'm sure you can relate to this sentiment. But, as I mentioned, this "Bunch" came with no "Alice." So, Wayne and I went to work. We posted **weekly dinner menus** on the fridge so I never had to think about what to cook and the kids never had to ask, "What's for dinner?"

Having set menus meant that **monthly grocery shopping** was the best use of time. The kids were involved with this process and we made it into a sort of outing. These adventures were supplemented with weekly grocery stops for perishables.

I quickly realized that older kids were at an age where both the time to primp and extra sleep had become more valuable than having breakfast. So I ditched the hot stuff (and the frustration of uneaten meals and wasted time) and went to nutritious things they could **grab and take**. Once I got over the very Brady notion that all of us should start the day together conversing over a good, hot meal, I reveled in the extra time.

I should mention, too, that **the kitchen "closed"** at a specific time on school nights, at which point dishes were not to be used. This was in order to preserve the sanity of the dishwasher du jour and also to be sure the kitchen was ready for the next morning's beehive of activity. If snacks were to be had, a piece of fruit, popcorn, pickles, or any other "finger" food would suffice.

Chores—Divide and Conquer

I decided to employ a model that my dad had used for me and my siblings when we were younger called **Rotation**. Tim was already responsible for the garbage and for helping Wayne with the yard work. So, I divvied up the common areas of the house (living room, dining room, den, kitchen, bathroom) and parceled them out to the kids for cleaning. This meant that each child had one room to be responsible for each week. At the end of the week, after a Saturday inspection, they rotated which meant that everyone got an even shake. This was a fabulous plan in many ways, except for one thing: I allowed the kids to do their own inspections, which a college-aged Gabbie later told me was, and I quote, "a *terrible* idea!" In retrospect, I agree. Sometimes, personal vendettas were involved between the kids and one would refuse to take the room from the other citing that "speck" on the floor. I recommend that a parent be the one who has the final say about whether the room is clean enough to be fairly passed along. Also, this easily enables teachable moments on cleaning and expectations.

Laundry Days—Wash, Dry, Fold, Repeat

Laundry was a real learning experience for me. I automatically assumed that the mom was supposed to do laundry—another unexamined, cultural supposition. Initially, I put bins in the laundry room and a hamper in the kids' bathroom. All they had to do was to bring the hamper into the laundry room and I would do the rest. Clothes would be washed, dried, folded, and put into their respective bins. They were to take the bins daily and put their clothes away. Reasonable plan, right? Not so much. As it turned out, they rarely emptied their bins and would come to the laundry room to dig out what they needed at the last minute (sound familiar to anyone?). In their haste, they would sometimes spill clean clothes into the dirty ones. I knew we had to come up with a better system.

It was at this point that I read about the benefits of kids being allowed to take on tasks once they were able to do them for themselves. So I taught them how to properly work the machines and gave them their own, personal laundry hampers to go in their rooms. They were each assigned a **laundry day** and if they missed it, they had to wait until the next week. Obviously, some weren't quite old enough to work the machines or to fold clothes so they got a little help, but they were a part of the system, nonetheless.

Years later, John was putting his clothes in the washer and grumbling to me that he was the only 10-year old he knew who did his own laundry. I told him that I did not think bragging was a very becoming trait especially for someone with so much natural talent and ability. At the time, he did not think it funny but now he smiles at the memory.

Depending on the child, age 9 or 10 is usually an appropriate time for them to take full responsibility for doing their own laundry. I was amazed by how much personal power they gained by doing this simple task. They began to take care with how many things they wore in one day and they thought ahead to what they may need, or not need, to wear. The best part was when they finally got to college they were astounded to learn that most if not all of their school mates were clueless when it came to doing laundry. They had no idea which buttons to press or what clothes to include in each load. Because it was a very scary and intimidating prospect, my kids were able to trade this service (which had become so second-nature to them) for having things done for them like class notes typed out and printed or rooms cleaned.

The Saturday Bag—An Idea Mary Poppins Would Love

Like many of you, my mind worked fast and furiously all day long and into the night. I had lots of information in my head. Tactical, creative and worrisome thoughts all fought for space between my ears. So, for me, extra stuff was *extra stuff*! I always felt better when everything had a use and a place. Many of you know how wearisome it is to try to keep up with all the literal pieces of every day life.

To keep a busy house decluttered is to have everything picked up and put away every day. Right? Yeah, Right! Easy for Mary Poppins to say but one day's accumulation of backpacks, homework, toys, books, and assorted projects for active kids can beggar belief. That's why the **Saturday Bag** became an essential and integral part of our home life.

This is the way it worked: After the kids went to bed, I confiscated things that were left out in the common areas (kitchen, living room, dining room) and placed them in a large trash bag. On Saturday, our regular chore time, the contents of the bag would be revealed and anything they wanted to recover could be "worked off." In other words, I kept a list of extra tasks that could be done in exchange for their, toys, shoes, homework, etc. If they didn't care enough to salvage it, the item was donated or given away. Very simple. Very effective. And, it made school mornings infinitely less painful.

Of course, after I said "good night" to the kids, I gave them time to remember and recover things by going into my bathroom to wash my face or brush my teeth. I used to get a kick out of hearing them quickly sneak out into the living room to retrieve a forgotten item. Sometimes there would be several pitter-patter trips!

Streamline—Having Less Means Having to Take Care of Less

Get rid of things that you don't need! I read once that we are best served by keeping only things that are either useful and practical, beautiful, or sentimental. Everything else can be donated or shared. Even now, I am amazed by how quickly I accumulate things. I still don't know where it all comes from! I donate at least a bag a month to charitable organizations and I also use a consignment shop. One good way to know you have too much is when you find yourself needing more storage space. I also began to make a habit of replacing items in my closet rather than adding to the mix. In other words, if I buy a skirt, I get rid of a skirt, etc.

Hearth

After School—Meeting Them at the Door

It had only taken a few weeks of my getting home from work *after* the kids to realize this was not the best scenario. It took extra time after work for me to pickup John from daycare and when I finally got home, I was met at the door with things not as ordered as they could have been. Fortunately for us, when the kids started school that first Fall, Wayne also began a 9-5 job with the school district. This meant that I could go from full-time to part-time. While it would have been very helpful for me to continue to bring in a full time salary, we felt that my being home was crucial. My generous employer allowed me to work my schedule around the kids' leaving and arriving. Switching to part-time work meant John did not need full-time daycare and I could **get home *before* the kids** did.

Even though, the oldest was technically old enough to babysit, I cannot stress enough the importance of my being home when the kids got there after a full day of school. Everyone had news, they were tired but excited to talk about the day's events, or to go out and play with the neighbors. An adult being there to greet them offered a smooth transition, a chance to calm down and have a snack and talk about the rest of the day, to help with homework and, for them especially, security without having to figure things out for themselves.

For me, it meant that I walked into an empty, quiet house each day after work and had a little breathing room. I had a few minutes to gather my thoughts, change my shoes and begin dinner while waiting for the door to be flung open and run through. This allowed me to get a handle on who did what to whom, who needed what when, and all other news and information that rolled in on the after school wave.

Although this will be a gargantuan task for many of you, I recommend that parents try to create a work schedule that allows for someone being home when the kids arrive. For single parents, this may be a babysitter, trusted neighbor or grandparent. There are also many outstanding after-school programs at schools, churches, the YMCA and The Boys and Girls Club to name a few. The dividend of at least arriving home at the same time as your kids instead of after them is well worth the effort.

Being Together—The Friday Night Lineup

Busy families do well to make room in the schedule for time together at home. Even if it's **just 1 night** where the expectation is that everyone will be home for dinner. Nothing fancy is necessary, sometimes just a movie or game or project like baking or making something. Although it may not seem so when they are young and clambering at your heels, the time goes by so quickly and soon the kids are off doing their own thing with little or no interest in beating you at Monopoly. Corralling them when they are young is far easier and much more enjoyable if they know what to expect and come to look for it.

Like many of you, we were a family in constant motion. We did not watch TV at all during the week because we just couldn't fit it in with after school activities and homework and supper and baths and bed.

But Friday was a special time. On Friday nights, the kids came in much later from playing outside, quickly got their baths, and settled on the carpet in front of our old TV, waiting for the family-friendly series of sitcoms called, "The Friday Night Lineup." The sweet, soapy skin, the pj's, the clean, damp heads on pillows and blankets, the laughter and imitations that came from the silly antics of Steve Urkel—all of these things coalesced to create some of our most cherished memories as a family.

Celebrations—We Are The Reason

At our house, birthdays were a big deal and **all of us were involved** in making the celebrant feel really special. Special meals, posters, homemade balloon bouquets, crowns, personal projects and special gifts were created by all members of the family regardless of age or ability. At some point during that first year, I subscribed to Amy Dacyczyn's *The Tightwad Gazette*, at the time a monthly publication. Amy was a pioneer in many cost-saving and ecological methods that are common today. These publications offered a plethora of smart, practical, easy ways to cut costs and were especially helpful with economical and fun party ideas. Unlike Amy and her handy husband, I never did build a birthday party pirate ship out of leftover materials, but I did get plenty of ideas which helped create really good times and good memories while not breaking the bank.

One of the things I learned as a rule of thumb was that parties work well when the number of friends invited to parties correspond to the age of the child. This simply keeps costs down as well as over-stimulation (for both you and the kid!). Another way to celebrate is to send birthday treats to school. This requires that you check out school policy and the teacher's preferences in that area. It's nice to have your child celebrate with their classmates when presents aren't involved. Teachers will sometimes allow small honors for the child, like being first in the lunch line that day or allowing them to be the errand runner or bestowing other privileges that are prized by the class. Brownies, each decorated with a simple math problem equaling your child's age are really fun. Those store-bought little tubes of colored frosting were so easy to use in writing 2+5=7 for Quy's seventh birthday, for example.

As the kids got older, their need to have a party with friends naturally became more and more important. We began to have family parties, which meant we'd have cake and presents after supper around the dinner table on their actual birthday. Later, they would spend time with friends at the skating rink or amusement park, or other venue. Activities were dependent on their age and how much they wanted me involved. Above all, the focus on birthdays was on the person and their wishes and happiness.

Holidays—Creating Simple Traditions

When it came to holidays, we thought it best that the kids practice giving as well as receiving. Sometimes kids are at a loss as to what to give parents. I did not mind shopping but Wayne, on the other hand, experienced outright panic at the mere mention of a mall. It took only one birthday for me to realize that with limited resources and six people so sweetly excited to buy me presents like inflatable candy dishes or roses frozen in Lucite, something had to be done. So, in order to save myself from becoming the recipient of countless trinkets, **I bought my own gifts** and devised a plan for gift giving that worked for all involved.

Throughout the year, I began to pick up little things that I would like for myself but would not ordinarily spend the money on, like a cool key ring, cute slippers, a box of my favorite tea, or inexpensive jewelry that I randomly found on sale. Once I had six items, I'd give them to Wayne for safekeeping. As Christmas (or my birthday, or Mother's Day) neared, he pulled the glittering assortment out and allowed the kids to "shop." Some items cost more than others, which meant that there were varying degrees of tasks to be done to earn them. I got what I wanted and could use and the kids felt great about being able to honestly "buy" something that I obviously loved. Although, once I had to wear the decorative shoe clips that I'd bought for my plain pumps on my ears because Wayne didn't know what they were and told the kids they were earrings. But, basically, it was a good system. Wayne did not have to shop. Extra chores got done around the house. And, the kids were overjoyed to give me such nice gifts.

Wayne's mom made **Christmas pillowcases** for all of us, a tradition she started with Wayne and his sister when they were born and continues now with the great-grandchildren. These pillowcases went on our pillows the day after Thanksgiving and stayed until the decorations went back into the attic. These, coupled with the **personalized stockings** she also made for each of us became cherished parts of the holiday.

I have a friend who allows the family to open just one gift on Christmas Eve. They all know what the present is: their new Christmas pajamas. They get them every year and even though her kids are adults now, they still look forward to the new sleeping duds. All of them, including mom and dad don their new night wear, pop some popcorn, and watch their favorite Christmas movie. I love this idea!

As the years passed, Wayne and I realized that one day the kids would have families of their own and would not always be able to be with us at Christmas. This caused us to focus more on **Thanksgiving** as our "family" holiday once the kids started going away to college. We did not want them to ever have the pressure of having to choose between us and their in-laws, or between being safe in their own homes as opposed to traveling in winter weather.

I heard people complain at times about "having" to go home for Thanksgiving or Christmas and quickly realized that I did not want obligatory relationships of any kind, and especially not with my grown kids. Even though I love having them with me, when the kids went off to college, I encouraged them, gave them permission if you will, to feel free to go on ski trips or to visit with friends during the holidays. Wayne and I both had the expectation that college for them would be a time for travel and exploration, for spreading their wings and flying from the nest a bit. As it turned out, this worked like reverse psychology in that they were always bringing their friends home to *us* for the Holidays.

Wayne bought the kids small hearts of candy for **Valentine's Day** and they enjoyed making cards for friends and family. We also celebrated **Chinese New Year** with the traditional little red envelopes and special foods. Greeting the kids after school with an assortment of green snacks on **St. Patrick's Day** was always fun. Chau's birthday fell around **Halloween** and so we'd have costume parties. Our costumes were homemade which added to the fun!

Heart

Baths—The Secret Weapon of Parenting

You've probably been wondering why I've suggested taking a bath at the end of each section. Well, if you have been wondering this, my ploy to get your attention has worked! My hope is that you've been including this important step in your day. If you have, I can imagine that it has become important to you.

When I became a mother, I was 28 years old and had come of age in a culture that valued worry, exhaustion and busyness. Taking care of myself: my body, my mind, my heart, was not something I had ever been taught to do. Going to a spa or on a weekend trip with girlfriends were things I'd never considered. In fact I was somewhat proud of the fact that I hadn't taken a bath in years. I only had time in my life for perfunctory showers.

I was engulfed in a busyness that eventually became a health threat. It wasn't until the younger kids were teenagers that taking baths as a way of having time to myself was recommended to me. Now, it is the thing I invariably recommend to parents during our first session together.

When you think of it, every major world religion uses water as the symbol for making the soul clean. The universal solvent, it is an amazing medium as the work of Japanese author, Masaru Emoto, exemplifies. Emoto examines the reaction of water when it is exposed to music, among other things. But more than the spiritual and esoteric properties of bathing, my point is to give parents permission to **carve out time** for themselves as a daily practice.

Many parents sigh and breathe heavily and can't imagine taking time off, going on a small vacation or even going out for the evening. But taking a bath does not require leaving the house. It does require a willingness to put everything else on hold so you can answer the call to yourself. It will allow you to realize that all will survive without you; it can be done! Letting the family know that you'll be unavailable for at least 10 minutes will give you 10 minutes to breathe, to dream, to dwell in uninterrupted possibility. This simple, doable act engenders respect for the self which, in turn, engenders respect from others. What you are conveying is that you are important; you are saying that your time is important and that taking care of yourself is important whether they understand it or not.

Model Parenting—Listen To Your Heart Song

Initially, I could not see the value of self-care. I did not believe that I was to love myself so I *could* authentically love others. People in my circles were working all the time either at home, their jobs, or church. This puritanical work ethic became woefully tyrannical. I took supplements and energy powders, the newest concoctions on the market when, really, all I needed was rest.

In the same way, I was not encouraged to think about any personal dreams or goals other than those having to do with maintaining my family. My creativity found its outlet through redecorating or rethinking plans or repurposing items as a resource.

Many years into parenting, someone used the airplane model to explain to me how important caring for myself really is. In the case of a drop in cabin pressure, people with small children are always asked to place the oxygen mask on themselves first before placing it on the child. This simple illustration brought home to me the importance of caring for myself in order to be able to care for those I love and brought a major shift in my perspective.

But the real clincher and impetus for change came through my M.D. who was also my acupuncturist. I was going through a difficult time in my marriage and because of my own preconceptions and self-expectations, was unwilling to do anything about it. My doctor looked at me and asked, "What would you say to your daughters if they were in the same situation?" This was obviously a rhetorical question. We both knew the obvious answer. She added, "Because the truth is that you are being a role model and no matter what you're saying, **they're watching and ingesting what you're doing**."

I share this with you because I, like you, want my kids to follow their hearts; they have good, good hearts. So, I began to try to model that, to pave the way, even though at times it was uncomfortable and scary. To my utter amazement, by following my gut, my heart, all the way through winding and unknown paths, I ended up in the land of realized dreams and continue to push forward into my own truth.

A Merry Heart Does Good Like a Medicine—Make 'em Laugh

Yes, we gained lots of tips and tricks and insights along the way that relieved some of the inherent stress of having a houseful of kids. But, equally important, was the **laughter** that made it extremely enjoyable. We laughed at every possible opportunity, many times when it was not appropriate which made the situation all the funnier (usually).

This ability to laugh was passed down to me from my maternal grandmother. Grandma was herself an orphan who was raised in a Children's Home. She had ten kids, three miscarriages, and one child who died at the age of four. She did not come from a carefree life of happiness and ease. Yet, she had a soft chuckle which morphed easily and often into a breath-catching laugh. Her way was matter-of-fact and gentle. As a child, I was attracted to her laughter and to her acceptance of me. I always knew that any story would be met with interest and even if it was a sad story, she'd come around with a smile and a silver lining to think on.

My heart pauses here because I have worked with so many parents who were not seeing much to laugh about. Many parents will pick up this book or call me because they are desperate to help their kid. Let me encourage you to take care of your heart. If you are in this predicament, practice letting go of the worry for at least an hour a day. During this hour, call an old friend (cousin, sister, brother) whose history you share. Tell the old stories about the silly times you had in grade school, high school, on that crazy trip. Take the time to watch a funny movie. Listen to your favorite stand up comedian. Blow bubbles with a giggling child.

Mother Theresa said, "peace begins with a smile." And it has long been acknowledged that laughter is *the* universal language. Studies show that it is good for the heart and for the digestion, correlates with longevity and relieves depression. But whatever can be said of laughter, above all it brings us together. It bridges gaps and fosters ties at times when words won't do. It's a wonderful legacy to leave to our children.

Bottom Line

Home is a sanctuary for all members of the household. Parents are the protectors of this sacred space, a sanctuary for them as well. I once had a single mom in my workshop who kept taking on more hours at work because she couldn't stand to go home to the mess her two teenagers left for her every day. The kids had locks on their bedroom doors and were rude to her in every way, treating her like the maid and bankroll so she crept in after work, cleaned up the kitchen, and went to bed. Once she began to assess her own value (usually while bathing) and perceptions of her role as parent, she was able to make tremendous changes. These began with her packing away all of the dishes and buying paper plates instead of arguing about cleaning up. When the annual invitation to spend Thanksgiving at her mother's house came, she did not invite her kids telling them that she would miss them but she and their grandmother had planned a day of peace and thanksgiving which did not include disrespect and rude behavior. It all worked out in the end and the family did share the holiday together only after expectations were made clear. Of course you can see that this household was in utter and complete chaos; desperate times call for desperate measures.

Author and Radio host Doreen Banaszak explains in her book, *Excuse Me Your Life Is Now*, how to recreate your beliefs about the "buts" in your life. The "buts" are those things that stand in the way of your life being as you'd like it to be. "I'd like to spend more time with my teenagers *but* they are too busy for me." "I'd like to be more organized *but* I don't know where to start." "I'd love to get more sleep *but* I need the hours at work." Any change that you'd like to make will of course begin with you. Remember the adage, "if nothing changes, nothing changes."

A sk Yourself

What is it that bothers me the most about our home life? What would I like to see instead? What small changes could I make to move toward this?

T ry This

Take a look at your own personal space in your home. Put on your favorite music and clean out your closet. Pare down your wardrobe to those things you wear regularly or have for special occasions. Get rid of the shoes, the belts, the t-shirts that you haven't seen in years. Move on to your bedroom. Go through one drawer at a time. Remember back to your favorite colors and themes of childhood. Use these on your walls or in fabric. Create a space for yourself. Write about your progress or what keeps you from progressing. Make your way out into the rest of the house, getting rid of those things that your family does not need or want. Get rid of clutter in the kitchen, in the living room, in the bathroom drawers. Use your journal to explore ideas and creative impulses.

TAKE A BATH EVERY DAY! TWICE IF NECESSARY!

EPILOGUE

Parenting Is A Temporary Role That Leads to A Permanent Relationship

"If it is peace that you want, seek to change yourself, not other people. It is easier to protect your feet with slippers than to carpet the whole of the earth."

Anthony de Mello

This past Thanksgiving, I sat on the couch and watched my kids, all grown up and looking after their own kids who toddled around with ipads and Legos. Quy (now Uncle Quy) was on the giant beanbag in front of the fireplace studying his phone, per normal. He came across some entertaining media piece and soon his siblings, the girls all beautiful women with long black hair, and the boys, now men, were crowded around him. Gabbie, due soon with our eighth grandchild, held her rotund belly as they all erupted into laughter.

When Tim started college in 1993, Wayne calculated that we'd have at least one kid in college, likely two or three at a time, for the next seventeen years. At that point, 2010 (which didn't account for John's choice of continuing on to Graduate School) seemed far, far away. Now, with all of them college graduates and on into their adult lives for many years, it seems to have flown by in a whirlwind of ups and downs, of tears and laughter and unseen glorious surprises. In 2002, for example, our summer was a beehive of activity with Chau's wedding and the other five graduating from various levels of college, high school, and middle school. Weddings in England, Vietnam and New Orleans were to follow with family reunions, trips and moves and births in between and since. Looking back, I marvel at how we've gotten through so much, not all of it pleasant, with our love for each other intact.

It was an illusion to think that I could raise "ready-for-world" kids by age 18, watch them go off to college, and then after four perfunctory years, enter into what I considered to be a good, balanced, well-rationed life. The glimmerings of that truth had already been shown to me through the trials and tribulations of post–adolescents. But the thought that I would never cut the apron strings occurred to me as most things had, rather late. There was a time when the truth that my children would never truly leave my heavy, tired heart even when they left my house was too much to bear. I had not given myself time to think much beyond laundry and feedings. I could not see that I had taken on so much more of their lives than was good for either of us, that I did not know how to regain my footing in my own life while stepping out of the parenting role in theirs. I did not realize that I could be there, in their lives, without bearing the enormous weight of responsibility that I had inflicted upon myself unknowingly.

But I couldn't have avoided all of this worrying because I was not the *me* that I am now. As it was, my children suffered and they thrived. Like you, I was doing the best I could with what I had. I just wanted to do as Joni Mitchell sang and, "come in from the cold," but I did not know how. My kids were not finished teaching me yet. I was a slow learner but they were persistent!

Through the years, people have frequently suggested that I write our story. I was always surprised by this notion. "Do they really think I know what I'm doing here?" Of course I could see that our becoming a family is a beautiful and touching story. But this truth was rarely at the forefront of my mind amid the happy busyness and bumblings of my early parenting years.

"Did people think I was making all of this stuff up?" On the contrary, all of the implementations and lessons came to me in the nick of time. And sometimes after many nicks! I was not about to tout any perceived success. As far as I was concerned the vote was still out. Yes, the kids were coming along, they were fed, they were bright, they were clean, they were smart, they were funny, they were color-coordinated for family portraits. But! Anything could happen! I could still be proven a parental failure! "I'm no expert!" I would shrill to the admirers who asked me for advice or gave me accolades.

Chiefly because of my skewed self-perception (my mother thought the vote was still out on me as well), I would have none of it and became secretly annoyed by the suggestion of yet another impingement on my time. Write down our experiences, indeed. Really? And, when would this writing take place? I would grow furious at the notion that I had time to write down anything save a grocery list. To make matters worse, I read about a woman who got up at 4 a.m. to write her novels before she got her kids off to school and went to work. Instead of inspiring me, this made me feel worse about myself.

It never occurred to me to look at the sea of emotion that this particular subject of writing stirred up in me. Had I been self-aware or self-actualized, I may have seen that this had to do with my innate, and long ago stifled, bent toward writing. I have loved it always; it was my first reaction to life from a very tender age. When I was 12, my response to my older brother's death was to write his biography. My writings were published, read aloud or posted up, given props all throughout my school years. Yet no one had ever suggested I become a writer or told me that I was particularly good at it and that thought would certainly never have occurred to me. So I seethed, never questioning the irrationality of my profound frustration.

Now, I look back on my young self with sympathy and with admiration. I did not learn well from theorists and behaviorists at that point in my life. I learned from those in the trenches of parenthood. Watching others is useful, especially if they have what you want. Eventually, I learned very gratefully from people who wrote books about their experiences and from my courses in graduate school. At any given point in time, I learned only as much as my mind and heart were in a place to take it in, no matter how good the information or advice. I wanted what all parents want. I wanted my kids to have happy lives. I wanted to be a part of those lives. I was doing my utmost best toward this end.

People who knew us, you see, were attracted by our story. They were given hope that upside down lives could be righted. They weren't really looking at me so much as they were looking at us. They saw from the outside what my harried inside life would not allow me to see. My vision was also blurred by the constant fear of having a child die. I could not imagine my life without them so my talons went deeper and deeper with a fierceness that the kids, understandably, often resisted.

I think back to years ago when I was just in college. My sister was pregnant with her second child and was worried (it runs in the family). She wasn't worried about the usual prenatal concerns. No, what brought her to tears more than once was her conviction, her utmost belief, that she would not be able to love this second child as much as she adored her first. I've since heard this from many others. The love that we feel as parents is a shock. It's a surprise and often a terror to realize that we are capable of such fierce love.

Of course, my sister did love her second child and the third and the fourth, with a leonine love. Despite her fears her maternal passion had not been consumed by her first born, leaving her nothing left to give. It had been ignited, not consumed. This is a surprise for us all. For some of us, it's hard to imagine that our parents were this crazy about us at some point. I've heard people say that they're pretty sure no parent has ever loved a kid as much as they do their own.

Kids, when growing up, don't think much about their parents' love for them. Not being parents themselves, they have nothing to compare to this kind of love. They are getting on with their own lives, they need for us to be there, but they aren't focused on how much they love us. In fact, they're sometimes telling us quite the opposite. Very often, they don't understand our concern and attention.

This is why it's vital for us to maintain our equilibrium as we parent. You don't love your kid so much because you expect them to love you back in the same way, or do you? Why do you love them? What is it you want from them? In the beginning, they need you. This is true. But, as they need you less and less, it's respect and joy for the life of your child that will allow you to be able to expand and let go in appropriate measure.

When I watched that Thanksgiving scene with all my grown children wrapped up in each other's laughter, it evoked that time long ago when this same group lay in a huddle in our old spare room. They were not such a happy group then, and they certainly are not always happy with each other even now. Yet despite the trials and tribulations, the aggravation and disappointments they've caused one another both as children and as adults, I was struck by their intense connection. They've been through so much together. And, with spouses and partners and children in the mix, they are certainly continuing to grow and develop.

I enjoy watching the kids press on into parenthood and career choices. I am honored when they call for advice or to vent or simply to check in on me. I've learned to let them go and am involved at times with their learning to let each other go as they all walk the paths that their individual choices present. I have the privilege of witnessing the dance of their lives as they run into and step around old patterns that no longer serve them. It is a joy to see them becoming their best possible selves. But mostly, I love being with them. They make me laugh. They continue to assist me in my own developmental journey as I see how differently they view situations and each other. They are good for me and they are good for the world. And they give me grandchildren! They are attentive and loving parents. They are so far ahead of where I was at that time in my life in terms of their self-awareness.

In hindsight, of course, I would have done things differently. I would have been calmer, gentler, more vulnerable and trusting. All of that worrying was a cold existence but growing older and wiser, making it my job to learn more about myself, has proved to be a warm, comfortable coat. I realize many things now that I could not have known then except by walking the path I've walked. The same holds true for you as well. You are walking the path of your life, becoming the person that only you can become. You are your gift to the world, to your children and to yourself.

Resources for Parents

1001 Things Every Teen Should   **Dr. Harry Harrison**
Know Before They Leave Home:
(Or Else They'll Come Back)

An exercise in helping your kids learn to live without you.

Adolescence   **Hans Sebald**

This academic book is now out of print but is still available. It places the phenomenon of adolescence in a historical and cultural perspective.

The Birth Order Book   **Dr. Kevin Lehman**

A fun and informative take on the role birth order plays in our personality development.

Bluebird: Women and the New   **Ariel Gore**
Psychology of Happiness

An uplifting study of the real secrets of joy and whether it's at odds with the modern woman

The Complete Tightwad Gazette   **Amy Dacyczyn**

Fun and helpful advice on managing your money, time, and resources

Excuse Me But Your Life Is Now   **Doreen Banazak**

An inspiring collection of personal accounts regarding the ability to manifest the life of your dreams.

Mothering From Your Center   **Tami Lyn Kent**

Will help you access your core creative energy to connect with the sacred feminine.

Parenting With Love and Logic   **Foster Kline/Jim Fay**

A basic tool that I recommend to all parents of younger children.

The Road Less Traveled   **M. Scott Peck**

An extraordinary book about life and the art of living

Steering By Starlight   **Martha Beck**

A most helpful book in beginning to imagine and reconnect with the life of your own dreams.

To Kill A Mockingbird   **Harper Lee**

Because Atticus Finch's parenting style is worth it.

You Can Heal Your Life   **Louise Hay**

Louise Hay has shared her wisdom and experience with millions of people regarding self-love and self-acceptance.

www.wou.edu/tri/eec. The Education Evaluation Center at Western Oregon University is a fine team of compassionate professionals who can help with assessing needs for all ages.

YAR YOUTH AND ADOLESCENT RELATIONSHIPS COACHING

Terri Gregory is the founder of **YAR** and the direct service provider for one-on-one coaching and **YAR** workshops **for anyone finding themselves in a significant role in the life of an adolescent.**

"What I have discovered is not a methodology; it is a mindset. What we are talking about is a much researched and academically recognized supposition based on the stages of human life. My focus is especially on the adolescent stage. Understanding this stage and all of its implications allows youths to take charge of, and responsibility for, their own choices. For adults, it can provide a stop-gap, a way in which to look back and assess developmental lacks in personal identity. It is a means of pulling away from the dock of who we've become to launch into the waters of who we want to be."

YAR consists of intentional techniques that create an overarching mindset rather than a staunch methodology. **YAR** provides a delightfully workable strategy for helping adolescents develop the skills necessary to bridge the protracted and often painful gap between childhood and adulthood.

For more information visit **www.yarcoaching.com**

"YAR can be the difference between being a good person and being an effective parent."

About the Author

Terri Gregory is a mother, grand-mother, teacher, entrepreneur, world-traveler and lover of life. Terri is a professional educator, mother of 6, grandmother of 8 (and count-ing!) as well as a sought after speaker, facilitator and coach. She has extensive successful experience in both classroom and parenting roles.

Terri's wisdom and experience are superseded only by her generous heart and infectious smile. Her joy and passion is bringing the good news of relief and regeneration, especially to parents and teachers. Whether you are hearing her speak or reading her book, you will find comfort through her message and courage through her belief in laughter.

Terri divides her time between doting on her kids and grandkids, running her Bed & Breakfast in the beautiful Pacific Northwest, civic and community service, writing, speaking, and walking her dog Happy.

CPSIA information can be obtained at www.ICGtesting.com
Printed in the USA
BVOW03s1657271113

337541BV00004B/9/P